I0023145

George W Elliott

Tariff and Wages

Paul and his father have a dialogue discussion of these vital questions

George W Elliott

Tariff and Wages
Paul and his father have a dialogue discussion of these vital questions

ISBN/EAN: 9783337237097

Printed in Europe, USA, Canada, Australia, Japan

Cover: Foto ©Thomas Meinert / pixelio.de

More available books at **www.hansebooks.com**

TARIFF AND WAGES.

PAUL AND HIS FATHER HAVE A DIALOGUE
DISCUSSION OF THESE VITAL QUESTIONS.

*How Far and on What Basis a Protective
Policy is Justifiable.*

RELATION BETWEEN PROTECTION AND PRODUCTION
AND PRODUCTION AND WAGES.

IF A PROTECTIVE TARIFF DEVELOPS PRODUCTIVE POWER, IT
DEVELOPS THE SOURCE OF WAGES.

By GEORGE W. ELLIOTT, A. M.

BUFFALO, N. Y.:
MOULTON, WENBORNE AND COMPANY.
1888.

COPYRIGHT, 1883,
BY
GEORGE W. ELLIOTT.

TO

H. H. WARNER,

OF ROCHESTER, N. Y.,

WHO LAID THE FOUNDATIONS OF HIS FORTUNE IN A STANDARD
TRADE, THUS ILLUSTRATING THE ADVANTAGES AND
AWARDS OF LIFE UNDER THE AMERICAN COM-
MERCIAL POLICY, WHO HAS EVER BEEN

ONE OF THE MOST LIBERAL PATRONS OF WAGES EARNERS,
AND AN ARDENT ADVOCATE OF THE AMERICAN
PROTECTIVE POLICY,

This Book is Dedicated,

WITH THE PERSONAL REGARD OF

ROCHESTER, N. Y., June 25, 1888.   THE AUTHOR.

NOTE.

Moulton, Wenborne & Co., Buffalo, N. Y., have just published " TARIFF AND WAGES," by Geo. W. Elliott, of Rochester, N. Y. Mr. Elliott has had, as manager of advertising and publications of the immensely successful house of H. H Warner & Co., who have branches all over the globe, unusual advantages in the study of international trade policies. He withdrew from active journalism ten years ago for the purpose of making a study of trade problems. He was originally a free-trader, and is one now theoretically, but he believes, as an American, one must sustain a genuine protective tariff policy. He treats his theme in dialogue manner with his son PAUL, and makes a book so simple that the perplexing problems of the tariff can be readily understood by the wage-worker. He holds that there is no such thing as a fixed wages fund apart from protection, which is the source of all wages. He shows that protection does foster production in many respects that would not obtain were we in open competition with free trade England, and hence protected production, by furnishing diversity of employments, maintains a better rate of wages than could prevail were varieties of employments less numerous and were more labor forced into agricultural pursuits.

CONTENTS.

WHILE as a theoretical free trader I cannot justify an exorbitant tariff, I do believe in a judicious tariff, and in the pages which follow I have tried as simply as possible to explain in homelike conversation some of the reasons why a properly regulated protective tariff is justifiable from an American point of view. I recognize it as a policy, not as a principle of universal application, and admit that while it may be justifiable as a policy for the United States, it may not in the present state of her development, be the best economic policy for Great Britain.

I hold that wages begins and ends in production, dissenting emphatically from the theory that there is such a thing as a fixed wages fund apart from production. If the former theory prevails, there is a universal stimulus to an increase of production; if the latter be true there must be constantly a tendency to restrict the number of workmen so that each one may have a larger part of this so called fixed fund. Under one theory there must be, other conditions being favorable, a vast increase of prosperity; under the latter, a constant repression of production with consequent stunting of growth.

I admit that a protective tariff is an apparent taxation of the many for the seeming benefit of the few, but show that in reality, under a properly regulated tariff, the benefits derived by the many are greater than those derived by the few and exceed by many fold, in the long run, the general taxation imposed by a protective tariff.

I do not discuss individual cases. I try to confine myself to the general principles of the policies under examination, and to state principles briefly without extended elaboration. I do not believe that a protective policy is justifiable simply on the ground that it maintains what is called the high rate of American wages,—that is merely one of the many general benefits which it distributes among the masses and is an argument against the theory that a protective tariff is "taxation of the many for the benefit of the few." Whatever helps to distribute the profits of production among the greatest number of people is a salutary anti-socialism tonic.

The papers forming the chapters of this little book were first written in 1885, and published serially in the *American Rural Home* of Rochester, N. Y. They have been rearranged and extended and are published in this form in the hope that they will attract the interest of young men, on whose clear understanding of the simple principles of the questions now so generally absorbing the attention of the American people so much of our political future depends.

ROCHESTER, N. Y., June 25, 1888.

PART I.

CHAPTER I.

THE TRUE THEORY OF PROTECTION.

Natural Law does not Prevail in the Commercial World — A Theoretical Free Trader, as an American is a Protectionist from Force of Circumstances — Selfishness the Law of the Commercial World — Human Institutions developed by individual Self-sacrifice — A Protective Policy, based on mutual Self-sacrifice, for the Greatest Good of the National Community is Justifiable — The Growth of Society, the Development of Trade and Manufactures, and the Demand for Protection — Limitations.

SCENE: *Sitting-room of a thoughtful, studious farmer. Paul, the son, having been graduated from college where he has been filled with unqualified free trade notions.*

PAUL: Father, I heard a man in the post-office department at Washington talking very excitedly with another gentleman last week and he emphatically exclaimed: "I tell you sir that free trade is natural, protection is artificial and should be condemned by all intelligent people." Is free trade "natural" and is protection a restricting of what may be called natural laws of trade?

FATHER: Well, my son, your questions are rather sweeping but both can be answered with Yes.

PAUL: Then why hamper so-called natural laws with human restrictions?

FATHER: With true Yankee characteristic, Paul, I will answer your question by asking others:

Is land free?

PAUL: No, sir.

FATHER: Is water free?

PAUL: No, sir.

FATHER: Are human impulses free?

PAUL: No sir, not among civilized people.

FATHER: Is bread free?

PAUL: No, not bread but many fruits and forms of food are free.

FATHER: Entirely and universally?

PAUL: Perhaps not.

FATHER: Can one do as he pleases even under the freest democracy?

PAUL: No, I think not.

FATHER: Are political actions free from the control of law?

PAUL: No, sir.

FATHER: Are religious impulses free from legal limitations?

PAUL: No, sir.

FATHER: Are social impulses free from the restraints of law and custom?

PAUL: No, sir.

FATHER: Are commercial affairs exempt from the restrictions of law?

PAUL: No, sir.

FATHER: Is it not true then *that almost nothing is exempt from restrictions imposed by the selfishness, by the mutual interests and self-sacrifices or by the self-defensiveness of communities?*

PAUL: Well, sir, your questions are pretty hard for me to combat but it would seem as if you were right.

FATHER: Well, my son, the existing restrictions are imposed as the result of human experience and though perhaps some of the restrictions are too stringent sometimes and too long enforced occasionally, in the main they are wholesome and necessary. Free trade, as the gentleman so emphatically observed, may be "natural" but it does not follow therefore that it is best for every people under all and any circumstances. On the contrary *free trade, in the present state of society, is more an end to be reached by processes of growth and preparation than it is a condition precedent to growth and commercial perfection.*

PAUL: Don't you think that the world would be better off commercially if there had never been any restrictions on trade?

FATHER: A rather extensive question, my son, which might require volumes for a complete answer, but I may say that a protective tariff has been the rule,—*that selfishness is the mainspring of all commercial enterprises, and that a tariff is a true out-*

growth of human selfishness. It is therefore an open question if the world would have been as well off—that is to say, if as satisfactory conditions would have been as well distributed as they now are—had there never been any artificial restraints on trade. It also seems to be a law that *progress is from a tariff more or less high unto free trade.*

PAUL: Then why not help along the car of progress by at once urging the free trade theory?

FATHER: UNDERSTAND ME, my son, I AM THEORETICALLY A FREE TRADER but PRACTICALLY, *as an American, giving full consideration to our commercial and industrial circumstances,* I MUST BE AND AM A PROTECTIONIST. Free trade is the keystone of the arch of commercial development, and *you must raise your arch before the keystone can be set into its place.*

PAUL: According to your theory, father, only the oldest and best-equipped commercial powers can be free traders.

FATHER: In general terms that is my belief, unless the whole world practices free trade.

PAUL: If that is the fact you have the floor, father, for a full explanation of your theory.

SOCIETY RESULTS FROM SELF-SACRIFICE.

FATHER: Very well, my son; now for my ideas.

Society is an association of men who obtain by mutual self-sacrifice what would otherwise be unattainable by the mass. *From a politico-economical standpoint society can exist only on the basis of self-sacrifice for the greatest good of the greatest number.* There are very many ways in which individual concessions make for the public good and no argument is needed to emphasize the importance of such concessions. Society is necessarily a curb. It is a hedging about of individual impulse by public will. The liberty it affords is in the direction of those things which the public will has determined are for the best interests of the greatest number of people, and this liberty, its amount and kind, depends upon the widest intelligence for determining what shall be the public will.

Society, furthermore, may be described as *diversity in unity.* That is to say, there are all sorts of men and interests concerned in the formation of society and the greater the diversity of mutually harmonious interests and the stronger the economic unity the more advanced and prosperous, as a rule, will the society be.

THE GROWTH OF SOCIETY.

Take, for instance, one hundred families first landed and settled in rude cabins in a new and strange country. Fertile Land abounds on every side and willing Labor pays hopeful homage to its generous patron. Agriculture—productive labor on land—is the basis of all wealth and in a new community most of the people become agriculturists from necessity. In a few years if prosperity attends them the labor spent upon the land yields more than the necessities of life call for, and then the people are able to exchange their surplus, if transportation means be at hand, with older communities, getting in return therefor better articles of household comfort, better clothes, better homes, richer carpets, libraries, papers, than they could produce.

With increase of the products of labor comes the desire for a betterment of the condition. The sons and daughters of the farmer are given an education, and to the gratification of their parents seem qualified by natural and rudely-cultivated gifts to excel as mechanics, artisans, musicians. They return from school to the farm but they find farm life both irksome and uncongenial. Bear in mind that at this time nearly every one is a farmer, and, indeed, the tilling of the soil is the only means open for the gaining of a livelihood.

DEVELOPMENT OF TRADE AND MONEY.

What now is most needed in order to introduce that diversity of employments and vocations so essential to a substantial society? It is as impossible that all can be farmers as that all can be preachers, or artists, or lawyers, or merchants or mechanics. Natural and cultivated ingenuity gives one man excellence in some one branch of rude manufacture, and eventually we find him depending for his living on what he can gain in grain from the farmer in exchange for his products of the soil, or for the mechanism of his hands. This is *Barter*—an exchange of commodities for other commodities.

Eventually some go-ahead wandering sort of Arab discovers precious metals and in the course of commercial evolution this metal is run into what is called *Money;* then the mechanic in dealing with the farmer does so not directly face to face but he takes his wares to a third party who rewards him, not in wheat, corn, and oil, but in this article called "money." It, too, is a commodity—the product of labor expended on land—but it is more convenient than wheat, corn and oil because it can readily and universally be exchanged not only for wheat, corn, and oil, but for clothing, shoes, "gospel privileges," and other necessities and luxuries of body and soul.

The merchant originally exchanged commodity for commodity but when valuable metals were produced and, of certain size, fineness and weight, became a measure of value, it is plain that the value of all exchangeable articles in a community could be rendered to buyers and sellers much better by means of this metal than by trading wheat for corn, or corn for oil, etc. That is, if wheat equals X. and corn equals X., X. could always command at the will of the one having it whatever of wheat and corn might be wanted.

In this way what we now call "money" became both an alphabet for the expression of what various producers wanted for their products, and what those products thus "price-marked" were really worth in other commodities—in other words, *money became a measure of commercial values and a medium through which products were exchanged.*

THE MERCHANT CLASS.

With the introduction of "money" into society sprang up what we call the middleman—the one who takes in wheat, corn, oil, etc., from Tom, Dick and Harry, giving them money therefor, and disposes of them to others, taking money or its equivalent in exchange.   This middleman is the grocer, dry goods dealer, marketman—Merchants.

Now our primitive society originally composed of soil tillers has developed the *mechanic and the merchant.*   In the same evolutionary manner, out of the necessities of the developing civilization come with proper encouragement all the other divisions of labor and diversities of employments until finally *we have that variety in unity which is so essential to a prosperous society.*

SELF-SACRIFICE—TAXES.

With constantly growing development the county is divided into towns, the town develops into the village, the village into the city; then for the common defense and protection come sanitary improvements, good roads, well-graded schools, public parks, gas, water, sidewalks, fire and police watchcare; every property-owning citizen sacrificing a certain amount of his income which he deposits in the common treasury for the greatest good of the greatest number.

The element of self-sacrifice enters into commercial relations as soon as barter commences. When the merchant is developed each producer apparently sacrifices a little and is willing thus to do because he appreciates the convenience of a middleman in the transaction of business. He makes this self-sacrifice unwillingly at first because he thinks that he could just as well as not save what the middleman makes for acting as the intermediary, but a little experience teaches him that in the end he gains more by using the middleman's skill and special training than he would by ignoring them. Likewise, equitable taxes judiciously expended, he learns by experience are a blessing and they are at length willingly paid *though they never return to him in kind.*

DEVELOPMENT OF CAPITAL.

By and by as a result of prosperous labor and a fertile soil there is an accummulation of money in the community—Capital it is called, the surplus or unconsumed product of labor on land. This is laid by and they who possess it seek opportunities so to employ it that it shall return them an increase —Interest. But opportunities are scarce. Abundance of unemployed capital is not a blessing. In many cases they who have this accumulation are too old or are otherwise unfitted for manual toil and unless they can invest this capital so that it will return a revenue, they will soon consume it and become dependent upon the public. *Capital like land is valuable only as it is productive.* But the resources of the community have been devoted chiefly to grain raising and the rude manufacture of what is needed by the people of the community. With its greater development better things are wanted. Coal and iron are discovered and there is a desire to establish a foundry and a plow works.

One hundred thousand dollars are raised and operations are begun. In a few years every cent is lost for other and older communities richer in men and means capital and skill, and having cheaper as well as better labor have been able to produce iron manufactures cheaper and better than they can be made in our young community, and the venture is a failure!

What shall be done?

A PUBLIC MEETING.

Must we always be tillers of the soil? Is there not *some new form of self-sacrifice* that we can make for the greatest good of the greatest number? *Is it possible that we cannot develop and maintain a home market?*

A public meeting to discuss ways and means is called, and is largely attended. JOHN GOODDEED makes the following address to the interested audience:

THE TRUE THEORY OF PROTECTION.

Fellow Citizens: I am a married man. I have a thrifty wife and three children. Twenty years ago this entire country was a bleak wilderness and was as unpromising apparently as is our ill-starred foundry. We worked hard, sacrificed every unnecessary comfort and many desirable ones so that we could accumulate something for old age, but it has all gone up in that venture!

As I said before, I have three children. Some one may say, "Why did you have children? They are a burden and expense?" Certainly they are an expense but I deny that they are an unrequited burden because the comfort one takes with them, the love with which they repay all our sacrifices infinitely recompenses every other consideration! Children are a necessity and self-sacrifice for them is a necessity; every member of my family counts it a joy to deprive himself or herself of whatever will contribute to the happiness and well being of the dear children. This is in accordance with the laws of nature, and, God bless you, *nature rewards*

*us for every sort of self-sacrifice made to feed,
clothe, nurse, educate and prepare these children so
that when they become independently-equipped men
and women, they will be able to fight their way
through life on an equality with other men and women.*
They enter society and are governed by the laws as
they find them—they are free only within the law.
Until they are of age and able to look out for
themselves we look after them, always having in
mind that the aim should be to *prepare the child
for independence when the age of responsibility is
reached.*

Now then, with this familiar sort of illustration
I beg leave to present this plan of *Community Self-
Sacrifice* by which I believe our manufacturing
industries can be sustained during the developing
period until they are able to bid defiance to all
outside competitors.   After that point they have
no right to exact a tax from the community for their
own benefit ; if such tax is then imposed it is legalized
robbery.   I think that it is not only perfectly justifiable but also absolutely necessary that we should
*meet the advantages possessed by our older and better
equipped foreign commercial rivals by some sort of
protective tariff,* and my plan is this:

It costs us, say, ten dollars to make a plow. We
want 25 per cent. for profit and contingencies, and
we sell the plow for $12.50.   But England is able
because she has the skill and means to make a

plow better than ours, transport it hither, and put
it on our market for $10. Is it any wonder that we
cannot maintain our plow works? [No, no].

Now I hold that this plow works sustains the
same relation to this community that the dependent
child does to its parent, and under all the circumstances we cannot be prepared to compete with
the older and better foreign plow works unless we
as a people take our own works to our hearts and
sacrifice something on its behalf, a sacrifice, however, that is more apparent than real, for *self-sacrifice is a duty we owe the family and the community,
and the reward is as a rule greater than the sacrifice.*

My plan therefore is this: Compel the foreigner
to pay such a sum for the privilege of bringing his
plow to our market as will make it possible for us
to establish and maintain our plow works at a
reasonable profit. In other words *a tariff gives
us advantages that otherwise our foreign rival would
possess to our detriment.* [Applause]. I therefore
recommend that a tariff of thirty per cent. be laid
on the foreign plows. This will give us an advantage of five per cent. and in a few years we shall
have prosperous plow works and, continuing the
policy to other industries, in the diversity of employments thus secured we will find openings for
capital and all sorts of work for all sorts of skilled
workmen.

Understand me, *I would not have this tariff a*

perpetual one. As our capital, skill, resources
and experience increase, and we can produce
plows cheaper and better, I would have the
tariff correspondingly and gradually decreased, and
when we could safely do so I would remove it
entirely and say to the plow manufacturers, as I say
to the fully-equipped man or woman—"*Paddle
your own canoe.*" This is what I call the true
theory of a protective tariff. [Prolonged applause].

THOMAS DOUBTFUL addresses the people, say-
ing;

"DOWN ON THE TARIFF ROBBERY."

Fellow Citizens: I am a farmer. Eight hundred
of the 1,000 men in this settlement are farmers.
We have wrested wealth from the soil by hard
labor and for one I am opposed to this tariff. I
can now buy plows from abroad for $10 each. Sup-
pose that every one of us 800 farmers wanted a new
plow. Under this tariff we would have to pay at
least $12.50 each for them, or $200 more than they
would cost without a tariff, and I am totally
opposed to it—*it is robbery of the soil-tillers for the
benefit of the manufacturers.* I prefer never to have
manufactures in this town rather than to be compelled to contribute $2.50 for the privilege of hav-
ing plows made here. How much richer is the town
under such a plan? Suppose that we cannot make
more than enough plows to supply our own town.

Suppose too if we could that all other markets were closed to us by local tariff, thus cutting off our surplus market, each plow buyer has given $2.50 for the maintenance of a plow factory and nothing has been added to the total wealth of the community. Away with this tariff delusion, I say! It is "robbing Peter to pay Paul." [Applause.]

JAMES INSIGHT rises and says: *Mr. Chairman:* I like Mr. Gooddeed's plan. Now then suppose that there were $100,000 in this town, and of the thousand people ten persons were worth, all told, $90,000. Let me ask the last speaker if he would not consider that scheme beneficial to all the people which would help to a *more even distribution of this money?* Now, I hold that wealth in the hands of the few is not the benefit to a community that wealth is in the hands of the many, and *I believe that manufactures would facilitate the distribution of our wealth by keeping it more constantly in circulation.* Certain persons have what is called capital. We are raising now all the grain and vegetables we need, and more capital invested in farm work will overstock the market and the agriculturist will soon be unable to effect exchanges at a profit. Every farmer has all the help he needs now. What, then, is to become of the fifty mechanics amongst us? Shall they become town poor to be sustained from the poor tax? It will cost at least two dollars a week to support them in idleness. If they can earn no money for bread they may become desperate with hunger, and from want plunge into crime. If our plow works can give them employment and we do have to contribute $2.50 for every plow made it would be cheaper in the end than to care for them out of the poor fund, for that would cost $5,250. Whereas, if every one of the 800 farmers here bought a new plow this year, at $12.50, they would be contributing a total of $2,000 to the sustaining of an independent manufactory in the town. The wooden material for the 800 plows would cost, say $1,000; the iron work, $2,500; the wages, $6,500; total, $10,000. By this division the fifty mechanics get $2.50 each a week. Without this tariff they get nothing whatever, our local exchanges are limited, and we have to put our hands in our pockets and pay out at least $2 a week for their support. For one *I am in favor of the tariff and shall vote for it because it promises to keep the sixpence nimble, to furnish employment for the mechanic, investment for the capitalist, and an equitable distribution of wealth, without, so far as I can see, doing any one any unrequited harm.*

Robert Freetrade—*Mr. Chairman:* I insist that you are robbing the soil tiller for the benefit of the manufacturer without any adequate return and I protest against it. If I give $2.50 more for

an American plow than for a foreign one, where
am I to look for my $2.50 from the manufacturer?
It is stated by my friend here that I get it back.
How? When? Where? Does the mechanic pay
me any more for my grain and truck? Not a cent.
If he works and earns $2.50 he pays $2 for what
he eats. If the town takes care of him, it costs,
it is said, $2 to care for him, or about the same
thing, so in either case there is the same demand
for what I raise, and I am, under this tariff, out
my $2.50.

Mr. Chairman, said Mr. COGITANS, my friend is
in error *in expecting returns in kind.* We are taxed
for gas, walks, roads, schools, fire and police protection, and our taxes are money. *We do not get money
back, but we do get* (what we esteem as better than
the money; we vote for it or we would not consent
to be taxed) *light, good walks, good roads, schools,
protection from fire and criminals.* Because we do
not get directly, like for like, it does not follow
that we do not get full satisfaction for all our self-
sacrifice for the public good. *As I look upon this
tariff, it is in general like our taxes, a part of
wealth or income which each one pays to the state or
society for that which otherwise he could not have.*

As for robbing the agriculturist for the benefit of
the manufacturer, I may say that on precisely the
same grounds we may affirm that *every industry in
the world has been built up out of money wrested from*

land and labor, for land and labor are the original factors of all wealth, and if the plow works tariff is a robbery, men have been robbers almost from creation's dawn.   If I may quote precedent, all human history justifies the position we take, that *every advance in human progress has been made on the selfish plan so far as the rest of the world is concerned, and on the self-sacrificing plan so far as each community is concerned.*

PAUL: Well, sir, what was the result of the discussion?

FATHER: A canvass was had on the 30 per cent. tariff proposition and it was carried by a vote of 700 to 300, every male inhabitant in the community being visited, and his position recorded. Within three months the blast furnace fire was relit and the manufacture of plows was begun. The foreign manufacturers made desperate efforts to compete successfully and for some time offered their plows *at less than cost* to crush out our works, but they finally gave up the contest. During the first year the furnace and plow works gave lucrative employment to all our skillful mechanics in iron and wood, and a fair profit accrued to the capital invested. After a few years the company found itself able to produce plows successfully against competition with a 20 per cent. duty and the tariff was knocked off 10 per cent. Eventually iron and coal were found in the neighborhood and this fact coupled with the other one that, as the community grew in age the facilities for providing the necessities of life increased, the necessities therefore being reduced * in price, the labor of skill mechanics was cheaper, and the cost of production was so much reduced and the experience and skill were so much advanced *that finally the duty was entirely removed from foreign plows.* Then the plow works was able, single handed and alone to meet competition from any source. *Longer to have maintained a duty against foreign plows would have been an unjustifiable exaction. A duty which is justifiable up to the protective point fosters a tyrannous monopoly when maintained beyond that point.*

PAUL: Do you follow the opinions of Gooddeed and Insight?

FATHER: Yes, my ideas are expressed by them in general. A NATION IS LIKE A FAMILY — MADE UP OF MANY PERSONS OF DIFFERING CAPACITIES, AND FOR THE GREATEST ULTIMATE GOOD EACH MEMBER OF THAT FAMILY IS EXPECTED TO SACRIFICE A LITTLE PERSONAL COMFORT AND INCOME THAT ALL MAY BE SO DEVELOPED THAT EVENTUALLY EACH ONE WILL BE AN INDEPENDENT FACTOR FOR PROSPERITY BASED ON SELF-RELIANCE. In

---

* NOTE.—The basis of wages is what labor can earn on land, and as there is a constant falling off in what labor on land might produce there is a gradual lessening of the nominal, though not necessarily of the purchasing power of, wages.

the constitution of society selfishness must prevail with each family as a family, and self-sacrifice prevail among the individuals of that family as individuals.

The comparison holds good with states and nations.

CHAPTER II.

THE LIMITATIONS OF THE THEORY OF PROTECTION.

WHEN A TARIFF IS UNJUSTIFIABLE — REGULAR REVISION ESSENTIAL — CAPITAL WILL NOT GIVE UP PROTECTION VOLUNTARILY — IMMEDIATE FREE TRADE WOULD PARALYZE ALL DEPENDENT MANUFACTURES — FREE COUNTRY AND FREE TRADE NOT COGNATE FREEDOMS — PROTECTION FACILITATES THE DISTRIBUTION OF ADVANTAGES AND WEALTH.

PAUL: Why is it father, that tariff duties are so many times maintained when there is no longer any reasonable doubt that the protected industry is able to "go it alone?"

FATHER: Simply because protected interests are often purely selfish and without regard for the people's interests they will employ lobbyists and "persuade" legislators—many of whom are unable or "unwilling" to see the real condition of things —*to maintain a tariff because it gives them a large profit*. A monopoly fostered by invidious legislation is an unjustifiable and cruel extortion and should not be tolerated. The people should insist upon *a regular revision of the tariff by competent persons*, so that no member of the community may build a fortune upon the *ruins* of other members of the community. *That is a wanton violation of mutual self-sacrifice, and becomes "legalized robbery."*

PAUL: Don't you think tariff tinkering by Congress is an injury to business?

FATHER: Undoubtedly it is an apparent injury, and an actual one when the revision is unwisely made or made for political reasons, but the very fact that industries are constantly being graduated to positions of independence must be considered, and when this point is reached the tariff must be cut off. To allow it longer to be maintained would be legalizing what has become a robbery. *Capital cannot be expected voluntarily to surrender the vantage given by a tariff. The tendency always under a tariff is to create or maintain an excessive "protection."*

EFFECT OF IMMEDIATE FREE TRADE.

PAUL: What, in your opinion, would be the effect of an immediate recourse to free trade?

FATHER: The immediate ruin of all our manufacturing industries that had not been developed to the point of independence!

PAUL: What effect would that have?

FATHER: It would throw thousands of men out of employment at once; this would overstock the labor market and as a consequence there would be a depreciation of wages everywhere; the products made by the cut off concerns would of course come

into the country from abroad at a reduced price,
but this reduction would not compensate for the
general paralyses that in all probability would ensue
for the next five years or until the people adjusted
themselves to the new conditions. Free trade as
I have said must be an end reached by gradual
development. To ordain it at once would disrupt
the commercial relations so seriously as to defeat
utterly desired results that might be realized by
gradual progress, as we are fitted therefor, toward
free or independent trade.

FREEDOM AND FREE TRADE NOT SEQUENCES.

PAUL: One of the leading free trade advocates
says that " we are a free country and should
have free trade"!

FATHER: Yes and it would be just as sensible
to say that because we have free speech we should
have free rum! The two sorts of freedom are not
sequences—one can prevail without the necessity of
the other. In all commercial regulations we must,
in prudence, *avoid sudden changes;* if we grow up
to free trade the growth will of necessity be gradual
and then as we steadily develop from the depend-
ence which the tariff is ordained to overcome, to
the independence which the tariff has made possible, no serious violence will be done to our commercial interests. If we had more "hard-headed"
business men in Congress, instead of so many

theorizing lawyers and scheming politicians, I fancy that tariff revision would not be as disturbing to business interests as it now seems to be and often is.

PROTECTION DOES NOT ENRICH THE FEW ALONE, IT DISTRIBUTES ADVANTAGES.

PAUL: Don't you think that protection *enriches the many at the expense of the few?*

FATHER: Yes, if the tariff be unjustifiably high, but if it be simply a protective tariff then the people reap as many benefits as do the "few." The trouble is my son that people look at results with very little philosophy. If our manufacturers gain wealth in business the man who judges only by what he can see, exclaims: "look at the bloated bond-holder, the monopolist, the one enriched at the expense of the many," etc., etc. He *sees* the successful man's wealth, but of the vaster amount which he has distributed among the people in both comforts of life and superior advantages in every respect he takes no account, and yet to this one man's work the entire country is indebted. Take the Bell telephone for instance. Prof. Bell was protected by a patent. Under it he has gained many hundreds of thousands of dollars. *The patent was worth nothing to him until it was worth many millions more to the people* in manifold ways than he ever made out of it. *In estimating results we must take account of the seen and unseen bene-fits.* The Vanderbilt system of railroads has made tens of millions for itself but it has also, I dare say, distributed scores of millions of dollars' worth of advantages to people all over the United States. Our country has been under a protective tariff quite continuously since 1789, and we had accumulated up to 1880 over $45,600,000,000 of net wealth, that being an average of over $800 per capita of population. In Great Britain, which has been a free trade country since 1846, there was in 1880 a net accumulation of $39,755,000, or a little over $1,000 a head. We have accumulated our wealth in at least one-quarter the time in which Great Britain has won hers. This shows that the wealth of the country under protection has not all gone into the hands of the few in this country, nor under free trade to the many in England. Besides the wealth-showing, instead of our people being mostly of the agricultural class as England would have forced us to be had her policy prevailed, over 66 per cent. are engaged in other industries which a protective tariff so essentially helps to develop.

B

CHAPTER III.

WHEN MONEY SAVED IN FOREIGN CONTRACTS IS A LOSS.

EQUIVALENCE OF EXCHANGES NECESSARY — BUYING IN THE CHEAPEST AND SELLING IN THE DEAREST MARKET SUBJECT TO LIMITATIONS — FREE TRADE BETWEEN THE STATES NOT A CONCLUSIVE ARGUMENT AGAINST PROTECTION — FREE TRADE A GOOD UNIVERSAL, BUT NOT NECESSARILY A GOOD PARTICULAR THEORY.

———

PAUL: Suppose that a construction company advertised for bids on steel rails for five miles of railroad in this country, that an English company offered to do it for $5,000, and an American company for $5,250. Would it not be better to let the contract to the foreigner; better, I mean, for the people as well as the construction company?

FATHER: *Not for the people unless the foreign company, which would take $5,000 out of the country, expended it in the country*—which it could not do unless it got all its material and labor in the country—*or in the products of the country, for otherwise there would be no adequate exchange.* If all nations were on a free trade basis and each one had special facilities for turning out products necessary for the others, then it would make no material difference where the contract was placed, for

exchanges of products would be more or less con-
tinuous and equivalent and all would be able to
share in the profits thereof. That is to say, if
England could excel in iron works, America in
cotton goods, India in corn and wheat, Russia in
timber and gold, France in silks and wine, Germany
in linens and hemp, Australia in wools, South
America and Mexico in silver and diamonds—all
more or less necessities to all—then under universal
free trade the field of mutual interests would be
larger, each nation would be more dependent upon
the others and international considerations would
prevail; but, inasmuch as free trade does not rule
universally and as every nation recognizes the
necessity of developing—if possible—a variety of
interests so as to give employment to the variety
of capabilities which prevails, *a contract cannot be
sent out of one country to another without marked
detriment, unless, as I have said, it brings about an
equivalent exchange of commodities.*

Yes, it is true that the American construction
company gets the road $250 cheaper by giving the
contract to English bidders, and that it gets the
steel rails in return for its money ($5,000), but I
claim that without an exchange of products between
the countries the loss to the community and to
the company is in the end greater than the amount
($250) saved.

PAUL: How so?

ALL INTERESTS MUST BE CONSERVED.

FATHER: Carry the illustration to the extreme. The older and better equipped country, if we had ten thousand 5-mile contracts to let, could as a rule get the contract. What would be the result? We would send abroad 10,000 times $5,000, or $50,000,000, *which would keep thousands of foreign workmen employed at the expense of an equal number or an equal productive force of American workmen and mechanics, unless, as stated, the foreigners by buying of us gave us a chance to recoup ourselves.* The result would be the ruin of every steel mill and railroad mechanic in the land, and unless the capital sent abroad came back to us in equal measure for our other products we would be commercially paralyzed. *The idea that we should always buy in the cheapest market and sell in the dearest is subject to very important qualifications, and does not apply unless the buying and selling markets have well balanced reciprocal relations with each other.* Every dollar sent abroad, unless it directly or remotely sends back an equivalent, is lost to us. For our $50,000,000 we have 50,000 miles of railroad, but of what worth are the railroads if the money of the country is all gone and no .exchanges take place to enable us to recoup ourselves? *We must look beyond the few dollars saved on the contract to*

see if in saving them we are not jeopardizing the
greater interests of the community at large.

FREE TRADE BETWEEN THE STATES NO ARGUMENT AGAINST NATIONAL PROTECTION.

PAUL: But Sumner and other free trade writers
state that the very conditions of trade obtaining
between the states is an argument for free trade
and against protective tariffs. Sumner says, page
9, in " Protection in the United States"; " If it
"be said that small states [new countries] cannot
"afford to trade freely with great empires [old
"countries] here are New York and Connecticut,
" Pennsylvania and Delaware. Why do not the
"great states suck the life out of the small ones?"
Again: New states, like Oregon and Idaho, with
no capital and in the first stages of culture,
exchange freely with New York and Massachusetts.
Again, to show that states relying on one industry
can afford to exchange freely with those having
a diversity of interests, he instances Pennsylvania
and Colorado, California and Nevada, any of the
cotton states, and any of the northeastern states.
What have you to offer to the contrary?

FATHER: My son, I want to emphasize the fact
that *if all the business in the world were conducted*
on the free trade basis then every country would hold
the same relations, commercially, that the states do to

each other, and each one would thrive on a free exchange of its special product with the special products of the others. *It would be death to any state in this Union to take a commercial course different from that pursued by all the others, unless it were the oldest, richest, best equipped in men, means and resources.*

For instance: Suppose that New England were as well equipped to supply the wants of the rest of the country to-day as England is to supply the rest of the world. Suppose, also, that all the states outside New England were under a protective tariff— standard or variable—would it not be the supremest folly for any *other section* outside New England to throw open its markets to free trade, unless it was on a substantial economic equality with New England? *If all the world did business on the free trade basis, then protection would probably be unnecessary for any one nation, but when the leading commercial powers have protective tariffs, then I insist that in the face of such a superior as England, as long as she* IS *our superior, it would be commercial suicide for us to put in practice unrestricted free trade.* This, I take it, is a sufficient answer to Prof. Sumner's objections.

SUMNER'S OBJECTIONS IRRELEVANT.

Sumner's illustrations, however, do not apply to the case as I view it. Moreover, if they did, the present condition of free trade between the states is enforced by constitutional provisions. It is a sequence of the "nationality" idea. If one state could erect trade barriers against another the harmony would be disturbed and the Union imperiled. This provision therefore was deemed expedient, in order "to form a more perfect union."

Again, it does not follow that commercially the states have gained more by the free trade than they would have gained had state tariffs been allowed. Mr. Sumner assumes that they have, but I cannot admit assumption as argument.

CHAPTER IV.

THE EVILS OF OVER-PROTECTION.

Too Much Protection a Great Wrong — The Raw Material Problem—Admit the Unproducable Raw Material Free — Community Self-sacrifice demands Satisfaction always — The Rule of a Tariff on Raw Materials.

PAUL: Can you tell me why it is that in the heavily protected industries of to-day there are so many periods of action and reaction, prosperity and adversity? Is not this fact a serious objection to protective tariffs?

FATHER: It is a decided objection to an excessive tariff. The moment you put a tariff on any foreign article greater than necessary simply to foster our own, then capital makes haste to engage in the manufacture of the article thus favored, because the high tariff ensures a heavy return to those who are quick to take advantage of the situation. What is the result? Before the tariff, say $100,000 was invested in a certain branch of manufacturing. After the high tariff, $500,000 is put into the business and the consequence is that five times as much of the article is produced, and very soon, men make such haste to "get their pile" that the business is overdone, the demand is exhausted and down come the prices.

Physicians tell us that certain drugs in minute doses will accomplish physical good. If the dose is increased it will do infinite harm. "If a tariff is a good thing"— say some unthinking ones, "we can't have too much of it." I do not concur. It is healthful and stimulating when limited to simple protection against ruinous competition — it is demoralizing and enervating when prescribed in greater doses than such circumstances require. As a rule the greater the tariff on any one article beyond this point, the greater and more disastrous are the fluctuations attending its manufacture, provided this manufacture is the privilege of any who wish to engage in it.

We must not condemn the true protective theory because outrageous tariffs have been enacted in its name. I fancy that if many free traders — so-called — and protectionists would come to a clear statement of their views there would be a very substantial agreement between them. The trouble is that pot insists on calling the kettle black.

PAUL: What do you do with those who would limit the tariff to such a figure as would simply supply revenue to meet the running expenses of the government?

FATHER: To be consistent with the free trade doctrine they cannot accept this compromise—they

must meet government expenses (as they are met
in the states) by internal taxation.   (See page 10,
Sumner's Protection in the United States.) I cannot imagine the shape, form, size, or purpose of a
free trader who consents to a tariff "for revenue
only," when that revenue can be collected directly
from the people (as it is, in the form of taxes), in
the states.   In this particular England is logical.
She opens her ports to all the world, taxing only
spirits and tobacco, but she exacts a thousand and
one taxes from the people — there is the stamp of
royalty on everything of value, and I am amazed
that this eternal payment of tribute unto an ever-
exacting Cæsar does not disturb the equilibrium of
British loyalty.   I do not care to quote statistics
here, but you can readily imagine how perfectly
the net-work of "inland revenue" encompasses
the empire when you consider how enormous are
the annual expenses of the British government.

THE RAW MATERIAL PROBLEM.

PAUL: Father, do you favor a tariff on tea and
coffee?

FATHER: Can they be produced in this country, or are any attempts made to produce them in
this country?

PAUL: Not that I am aware of.

FATHER: Then I would not put a tariff upon
them.

PAUL: Would you put a tariff on what is called "raw material"?

FOREIGN WOOL.

FATHER: It is hard to define "raw material," for what is the raw material of one man is the finished product of some other man. That is to say, the fine foreign fleeces which the American woolen manufacturer needs to make a cloth equal to the foreign fabric, should not be put in the tariff schedule unless there is a reasonable prospect that it or its equivalent can thereby be produced in our own country, for otherwise we handicap the American woolen manufacturer in his competition with the foreign cloth maker.

DOMESTIC WOOL.

PAUL: But how would this please the domestic wool growers? Would they not have good cause to complain that they were not sharing the mutual benefits and self-sacrifices you talk about?

FATHER: They would have no just cause of complaint because they would have no right to ask for a tariff on an article which cannot be produced in the United States.

PAUL: But if a duty were placed on the foreign-grown wool, would it not compel our home woolen cloth makers to purchase the domestic wool?

FATHER: It might, but the ultimate purpose sought would be defeated, for *with an inferior wool we could not make a really competitive fabric, and, to keep the foreign fine wool goods out of the market, we would have to lay a duty on them which would be contrary to the true protective theory;* for it would never, by any possible self-sacrifice, secure the end desired — *a piece of domestic cloth as good as the foreign article.* In other words, the domestic wool growers would be asking self-sacrifice from the rest of the country from which no adequately compensating return would be got.

PAUL: How, then, would the domestic wool business get any benefit from the protective tariff?

FATHER: We would put a duty you know on all forms of woolen goods. Only the finer grades of cloth would require the finer "raw material" wool which we could not produce and by admitting this free *we would enhance the prospect of ultimately producing an equally good article of cloth.* The manufacture of the lower grades of cloth, which we *could* produce equally with the foreign low grades (the wool of which we would exclude by tariff), would furnish an ample demand for the domestic fleece. If it did not we would not be justified in excluding the foreign finer grades when the coarser domestic grades could never answer the purpose. *A tariff, to be justifiable, must give a reasonable prospect of an ultimate satisfaction of mutual self-sacrifices.*

FOREIGN VS. DOMESTIC PIG-IRON.

PAUL: On the same principle, then, you would put pig-iron on the free list if there was no apparent prospect that pig-iron, good enough to place our iron products on a level with the foreign competing article, could be produced in the United States?

FATHER: Certainly.

PAUL: Then, accordingly, we must accept the alternative of free foreign pig-iron, or no possibility of successive rivalry of home made with foreign made iron products?

FATHER: Exactly. The *home* producers of pig-iron have no right to ask that the country be taxed for their benefit if no compensating return is even possible.

We may state the general rule that we must admit free of duty those products — "raw materials" if you please — which our manufactures must have in order that they may successfully compete in the home market with the foreign article excluded by a *true* protective tariff, *provided* that that raw material or what is equally as good cannot be produced in our own country, or, provided that we cannot make by superior skill or resources in manufacture even with a lower grade of "raw material," an article as good as the foreign made article.

THE RULE OF A TARIFF.

We cannot with an inferior "raw material" hope to compete with a manufacturer having a superior "raw material," unless perhaps we can gain compensating advantages in the methods and facilities of manufacture.

PAUL: Father, if we can make any article cheaper and better than any foreign manufacturer could, would you place a duty on any "raw material" entering into its manufacture?

FATHER: Not unless by so doing I could develop an equally good or a better raw material here.

PAUL: Suppose then the duty put on the foreign "raw material" should so increase the cost of manufacture that competition would be put out of question?

FATHER: I should proceed very cautiously, and would not put the duty on if I was sure that I would destroy well-established manufactures—it would be very unwise to exchange a certainty for an uncertainty—a thing attained for one possibly, if attained, of no greater value. *We are not justified in asking community self-sacrifice unless we can render a satisfactory equivalent therefor.*

CHAPTER V.

THE PROBLEM OF OVER-PRODUCTION.

Not Necessarily Involved Exclusively in the Tariff — Over-Production as much a Sequence of Free Trade as of Protection — Human Nature and the Question — The Tariff North and the Free Trade South in 1860-65 — We shall Eventually be Free Traders in Policy.

PAUL: To-day I met an intelligent farmer who writes much for the agricultural press, and he said that protection had injured manufacturing in this country and quoted over-production as evidence.

FATHER: Might he not as well have said that over-production was as much the result of the fact that our business men are too sanguine, rush pell mell into the mad race for wealth; that too many "nincumpoops" are trying to conduct the business of the land — men who put no real judicious thinking and planning into commercial transactions? An unjustifiably high tariff no doubt does injury — it is an overdose of a good thing — but it is a shameful calumny to attribute all our commercial ills to protection even though the tariff be higher in some respects than can be justified.

NOT NECESSARILY CAUSED BY PROTECTION.

Does not the same state of things arise in calm,

sagacious, cool, calculating, free trade England? It is not the system that is so much at fault as it is that the "business men" who are working under it are so ill prepared to fashion out a wise, conservative business policy. As long as people, like fishermen, rush to the most productive parts of the ocean of commerce, neglecting all the rest, we may expect an overdraft of fishes when a hundred nets are set where one should be. Over-production follows as much from want of business sagacity as from the fact of protection, and I think a deal more. Money in the hands of impetuous men rushes pell-mell where it can quickest increase upon itself. As a result it soon exhausts this source of wealth and what was once very profitable now becomes a source of loss.

DEVELOP INDUSTRIAL INDEPENDENCE.

My son, the American people believe that it is a good and desirable thing to be as independent as possible of all the world. During the late war the South, which had for years been in favor of free trade and did nothing to develop manufactures, was utterly exhausted. When all the foreign ports were closed to her by the Northern blockade, the source of supply of war munitions, clothing and all manufactured articles was cut off and four years of war impoverished her. Had the North been in like manner isolated she would have been able to endure ten times as long because she had developed diversity of interests and was able to manufacture nearly everything she needed. The free trade section was unable to cope with the protectionist section.

WHAT FREE TRADERS ADVISE.

Free traders want us to develop our natural resources and depend on the world's markets for all else we need. Protectionists insist that it is wiser to become a complete people, able to supply all our own needs in peace and war. We hold that our people should be masters of the details of all the necessary trades, whereas the free trader says: "Put the sole on the shoe, if nature has best fitted you for this work, but let some other nation finish it and put it on the market if it is best fitted for that work."

WHAT PROTECTIONISTS ADVISE.

Protectionists, however, say: "Raise the cattle, tan the leather, make the necessary lasts and machinery, cut, fit, sew, sole, finish, make a home market and sell the finished shoe yourself." I confess that I like the protectionist advice for our country, and am more than willing to employ legitimate protection up to the point where we can accomplish this complete development.

WE SHALL BE FREE TRADERS EVENTUALLY.

A nation that is thus capable, will some day command the trade of the world, and when that time comes, every self-sacrifice made to develop this independence will be satisfied. Some day when all the circumstances permit we shall be a nation of free traders with the majority of our industries. Every decade brings us nearer to the industrial independence that makes free trade possible here in all respects, and when we do properly take that position we shall commercially rule the world. Every year many industries under our fostering tariff become independent of the tariff and are able and should be required to push out on an independent career.

PAUL: Since you are a theoretical free trader how would you hasten that free trade regime?

FATHER: I would try to have an international commission appointed for the purpose of advancing free trade conditions throughout the world. Then we would take our chances with the rest, as each state takes its chances of trade with all its fellows in the United States.

PAUL: Would you favor free trade if it could be made universal?

FATHER: Yes, provided sufficient notice was given so that all the world could prepare itself gradually for the new conditions.

PAUL: Don't you believe if the United States should ordain free trade, that she and England would compel other nations to adopt it?

FATHER: No, sir. Free trade is an evolution, and it can never be accomplished by a spontaneous revolution. It will prevail in each nation only as personal experience shows that it is the wisest and best policy for each nation to pursue.

CHAPTER VI.

WHAT IS MONEY AND WHAT MONEY IS NOT.

GRESHAM'S LAW EXPLAINED—THE EVILS OF ANY FORM OF
DEPRECIATED CURRENCY SURE TO BE REALIZED—HONEST
MONEY POLICY IS THE BEST.

PAUL: Speaking of wages, father, we come first to the question of money. Will you please explain Gresham's law that "the baser money always drives out the better?"

FATHER: "Gresham's law" is quite axiomatic. If you sell an Englishman a plow for $10 you want exactly ten dollars and you want that ten dollars actually, not nominally. If England has gold and silver standards of money, and two gold sovereigns are nearer the exact measure of $10 than forty silver shillings, you will expect and can demand settlement in gold. If the forty English silver shillings are nearer the $10, you will demand forty English silver shillings in pay. Thus *in order to settle his debt the Englishman must send here his best (most valuable) money and thus the cheaper money, whether it be gold, silver or paper, drives out of England the better paper money.* Hence in all international trade the balances which have to be settled in money must be provided for by the medium that has the highest value in the inter-trading countries. In a few years, therefore, a continuous adverse balance will take all the most valuable money out of the country, leaving the depreciated money.

"PAPER MONEY," GOOD AND BAD.

PAUL: How about what is called "paper money?"

FATHER: Paper is not money, it is only a representative of money and can have no commercial value greater than what it represents, A piece of paper issued by a government is a commercial convenience. If it is convertible at the will of the holder into the valuable thing — the product of labor — that it represents, it is a much more welcome circulating medium than coin for reasons which are apparent. If a bit of paper is called a "dollar," unless it has taken a dollar's worth of labor to produce that bit of engraving, pulp and color, or unless it can readily facilitate an exchange of a real dollar's worth of labor, it is a travesty of money — it is a fraud.

If such "money" were made a legal tender for all public and private debts in the United States, Gresham's law would again tell us that either the gold and silver would be driven out of the country in settling foreign balances if there were any, or, if not, the gold and silver would be driven out of

circulation at home because of the singular habit
that people have of hoarding them when "paper
money" gluts the land. *Moreover, as the value of
money depreciates, prices correspondingly increase, for
however men may legislate, financial justice demands
and will enforce a satisfaction of values.*

FINANCIAL DEBAUCHERY.

As I have said, money — the measure of commercial values and the medium of exchange — is
taken *for what it is or represents* — not for what it
pretends to be. And paper must represent something that has the commercial value indicated by
it, otherwise it must in some way be discounted in
exchange. Whatever prevents the immediate real-
ization of what paper money represents, decreases
its value in exchange. If the government issues a
$5 note payable in five years, in every exchange
accomplished by that note the length of time
which the holder of the note has to wait for its
redemption is taken account of, and, — the probability of its prompt redemption being conceded, —
the purchasing power of the $5 note is correspond-
ingly affected. Business is an exchange of actual,
not of nominal, values, and no legislative body can
successfully compel men to exchange what they
know is commercially valuable for what they know
is commercially not valuable. A few years' riot of
"paper money," based on the promise to pay in

the remote future may seem to short-sighted people to be an era of commercial activity and prosperity but when the inevitable settling day comes in the utter and universal prostration we read the evidence of a terrible financial and commercial debauch.

CHAPTER VII.

THE MODERN COLOSSUS OF TRUST.

PAUL: What are trusts?

FATHER: A trust is a combination of men in
any one branch of business, made for the purpose
of controlling the market.

PAUL: How do they operate?

FATHER: If I understand their *modus operandi*
thoroughly, it is that, for instance, all the refiners of
sugar in the United States "pool their issues" so
to speak, and agree upon the amount of stock that
shall be put upon the market and the price thereof.

PAUL: Well, father, you say that you are a free
trader in theory but in practice as an American
you believe in a protective tariff. Do you not
think the tariff fosters the formation of trusts?

FATHER: No, I do not think that trusts are
necessarily the result of the true protective tariff,
for if free trade were ordained to-day the same self-
interest that prompts the sugar refiners of this

country to combine for the purpose of controlling
the American market would operate on a larger
scale and you might find the sugar refiners and
other classes of manufacturers combining with the
same classes in Great Britain, with the same
results.

PAUL: Do you not think that trusts are an
injury to business?

FATHER: Yes, if they destroy local competition
under our commercial policy and crush out the
small dealer.

PAUL: But doesn't the protective tariff destroy
competition? You say it is ordained for the purpose of enabling the American manufacturer to
be developed, when you admit that without the
tariff the English producer could come in and sell
his wares much cheaper than we could produce them
at home.

FATHER: Yes, I did say that, but the circumstances are entirely different. If we foster competition on the free trade basis, unless all the world
is under a free trade policy then we lose all the
benefits that I have enumerated as coming from a
diversity of interests and the development of vary-
ing capacities, which we could not have secured
had Great Britain been allowed to enter our markets
as an unimpeded competitor. The protective tariff
renders it possible, when our protected manufacturer
has arrived at a period of independence, for him

to carry on the most successful competition with all foreign rivals. The protective tariff for the time being limits competition *to* the American market with the American competing. A trust, however, limits competition *in* the market over which it exerts its influence to the detriment of *all* competition.

PAUL: But if free trade prevailed wouldn't it be possible for us to defeat these trusts by so letting in the foreign competitor?

FATHER: No, not necessarily, because as I have said, the self-interest which leads to the formation of the local American trust by American capital could lead to a combination extending over two countries and the effects would be the same or even worse.

PAUL: But you assume that all persons engaged in a like industry *would* combine?

FATHER: Yes, I do assume that, because if a trust is formed it is formed after mature deliberation and those who do not come in are "frozen out" of business.

PAUL: Is there no way in which this cutting off of competition in the local market can be prevented?

FATHER: Yes, if the parties who form such combinations are incorporated under the laws of a state the body from which they receive their incorporation will have authority to regulate and control them.* Trusts organized by the modern barons of plutocracy should be made to feel that they are responsible to the people and that *they cannot exact a sacrifice for which they give no sufficient return.* But I did not intend to discuss the general question of trusts. I simply wanted to answer your inquiry and to assure you that *trusts are not necessarily and exclusively a sequence of a protective tariff.*

---

* Since the above was written the following dispatch appears in the Associate Press telegrams: *Albany, N. Y., July 2.*--Attorney General Tabor has rendered a decision in the case of the North River Sugar Refinery and the Sugar Refineries Company to the effect that an action may be brought against the great sugar trusts. A violation of Section 163 of the Penal Code was charged in that the company combined with others for the purpose of advancing and controlling prices, and the Attorney General was asked to bring an action to annul the existence of the corporation.

PART II.—Wages.

CHAPTER VIII.

THE WAGES QUESTION.

Relation of Wages to Commercial Politics — The Source of Wages more Prolific in a New Country than in an Old one — Under Foreign Competition Wages must be Lower — The Evils of an Adverse Money Balance.

PAUL: During the presidential campaigns the papers are full of statements that free trade would cut down wages, and that protection maintains high wages. What is your candid opinion of these statements?

WAGES DEPEND ON PRODUCTION.

FATHER: *If there is no production there can be no wages*, if we accept Walker's theory that wages are paid out of the product of present industry (Wages Question, page 12 *seq.*) — and I think this theory the sound one. Therefore, *whatever creates or maintains production creates or maintains wages.* If free trade in England creates or maintains production better than protection did, then in England free trade is the better friend of wages earners. If protection in America creates or maintains production better than free trade would, then protection in America is the better friend of the wages earners. Opposite theories can produce the same results in fields where circumstances conspire differently. If we were to get upon the free trade basis in this country now, in order to compete at all with England *we would have to reduce the nominal wages,* or be content with less profit.

PAUL: I don't see why, for, by removing all tariff duties would we not take off so much from materials that we could save thereby enough in the cost of production so that we would not have to reduce wages? Free trade would, I think, stimulate production, and thereby create or maintain wages. Am I not right?

EQUIVALENCE OF CHANGES.

FATHER: By removing the tariff, we would undoubtedly in some things reduce the cost of production so far as materials were concerned. But not enough to overcome the superior skill, the greater capital and the better transportation facilities of England. Again, by removing the tariff, *all the expenses of conducting the government would have to be met by internal taxes, which would of course add to the cost of the necessities of life.*

WHEN WAGES MUST BE REDUCED.

Take some illustrations:

If England and the United States were both free traders to-day, and if both had equal capital, equal facilities, equal skill, neither would have the advantage where raw materials (raw for their use) were produced, so one could not buy these materials cheaper than the other. Both have equal skill and equal facilities for manufacturing, both enter an open market to sell their products. It is plain that on square dealing neither would have the advantage. If the cost of production could not be reduced in the purchase of the raw material, and if greater capital, skill and facilities could not be had, then *reduction of profits or of wages would be the only source whence one nation could get advantage over the other.* Then, that nation would gain the advantage which could secure equally serviceable workers at the lowest wages, or be content with the smallest profits, and, other things being equal, the older nation would win this advantage, because *wages are lowest in the oldest country whose interests are most diversified* and profits are also generally lower. That is, owing to the greater division of labor and the longer practice of economy, an English workingman could make what is equivalent to a dollar a day go further than an American workingman could, and English capital is contented with lower profits.

Much less labor expended on land will produce a dollar in a new country than can produce it in a long-settled country, and what labor can earn from land is the basis of wages the world over. But if the

American competing manufacturer reduced wages
below what the services of the men could win in
other kinds of work,—farming, cattle raising, etc.,
etc., he would *force them out of manufacturing into
the more productive employments, provided there was
mobility of labor.* This would spoil the prospect of
successful competition with England, and also
unless the manufacturer increased wages by reducing his rate of profit, production in America must
cease. If, moreover, he raised wages, competition
would be out of the question and manufacturing
would be an impossibility. If he cut down his
profits in manufacture, capital would withdraw into
the more profitable agriculture.

RELATIVE PURCHASING POWER OF WAGES.

But again, England is older, living (such as it is)
is cheaper there, she has more capital, she has better working facilities. She can buy foreign produced raw material as cheaply as we can, her home
raw material is as cheap as we can produce our
home raw material for our own manufactures;
therefore, if we equal her at all in the cost of production we must do it by *scaling our wages down
to the purchasing power of hers.* Then, if our
goods were as well made as hers, we might trust to
Yankee enterprise and shrewdness to match if not
to beat her in open markets.

In all discussion of wages, my son, you must

always remember that, if the foreign workman gets
5*s.* a day and the American $1.25 a day, they are
not necessarily on a wages equality, for the purchasing power of 5*s.* ($1.25) in the older country
is probably considerably greater than is the purchasing power of $1.25 (5*s.*) in the newer country,
and the "necessities" in the old country are less
and cheaper than are what are required as necessities in the new country. *It is not the relation of
nominal wages that we must compare, but the relative
purchasing power of wages.* Demagogues and one-
sided politicians carefully evade such a comparison
when by so doing they can "make a point"
before an unthinking crowd.

PAUL: You say reducing wages and profits
below a certain point would force American workmen and capital into farming, cattle raising and
other employments. What effect would such
destruction of American manufacturing interests
have on these other employments?

WHERE THE ENGLISH FREE TRADER WOULD PUT US.

FATHER: *It would make us dependent upon the
foreign manufacturer,* and we would have to content ourselves with pastoral and agricultural life
and such manufacturing specialties as we could
create   (Cairnes 396, 1st p.) This would reduce
diversity of interests, there would soon be a surplus of farmers and farm products, and, exchanges

being free, *the balance of trade, or the difference, which has to be settled in money, would probably always be against us, and that would not be a happy circumstance.*

PAUL: Why not? You do not think it an injury to a country that it has to send its money abroad, do you?

WHEN THE EXPORTING OF MONEY IS AN INJURY.

FATHER: The settling of exchange balances in money is *not objectionable provided that it is done with some sort of equality by all intertrading nations.* For instance, if America and England are traders, and England sells to us year after year more than she buys, we will be continually paying her a money-balance, and after awhile, provided we do not in trade with other countries sell *them* more than we buy and thereby reimburse our money coffers, we should eventually be drained of our circulating medium. Like as the farmer who owns 10,000 acres of land and has no surplus capital is "land poor," so,—even though having the equivalent of the money sent abroad,—we would be embarrassed for want of funds with which to transact business. *A man who is always exchanging money for goods will eventually be reduced to barter or financial embarrassment of goods.*

But we are digressing from the subject of wages and must return.

C

CHAPTER IX

THE DOCTRINE OF A FIXED WAGES FUND.

ONE FORMULATED IN COUNTRIES WHERE THE PERIOD OF
DIMINISHING RETURNS HAS BEEN REACHED — A DISMAL
AND UNPHILOSOPHICAL DOCTRINE — THE THEORY STATED
AND COMBATED — WAGES BEGINS AND ENDS IN PRO-
DUCTION.

PAUL: What do you think of the so-called wages fund theory once held by J. S. Mill and afterward abandoned by him and now advocated by Prof. Cairnes?

FATHER: I have read Cairnes with a good deal of interest, and before discussing the wages fund theory it will be best to state it as briefly as possible.

THE THEORY STATED.

The wages fund theorists hold that wages is paid out of capital — not out of the products of present industry. Hence they say that entering into pro-duction are capital, *fixed* (that is, the amount put into buildings, machinery, etc.) *circulating* — (that used for purchasing raw material and labor), and labor; if a man has $100,000 to invest in manu-facturing, he finds that $60,000 must be fixed in buildings, machinery, etc., leaving $40,000 free or circulating with which to purchase raw material and labor. Cairnes holds that a certain amount, regulated by the conditions of the labor market, of this free capital, will, according to the laws governing supply and demand, go toward payment of labor; if the raw material costs $15,000, labor will get $25,000; if raw material costs $25,000, labor will get $15,000; that the average wages of each workman will be found by dividing the amount set apart for wages by the number of wages workers necessary to carry on the business. If 50 men are required they would each average 1-50 of $25,000, or of $15,000, $500 or $300 respectively. More they could not get without compelling the manufacturer to convert fixed into free capital, less they could not get without compelling the manufacturer to convert free into fixed capital, provided in each case that the cost of raw material was relatively the same.

PAUL: What objections have you to this theory? Does it not seem plausible?

FATHER: My objections to the theory are as follows:

OBJECTIONS TO THE THEORY.

First: I do not think wages is paid out of the free capital. I think wages begins with production and ceases when production ceases and is paid out of the product of current industry.

Second: When one has $100,000 to invest in manufacturing, he estimates that he must put so much into buildings, machinery, etc., and so much into materials to work up into the finished product, and so much as a reserve to keep his bank credit good, to meet unexpected losses, and to provide for the wear and tear of machinery, insurance on buildings, etc., and *to advance from circulating capital for the payment of wages between the date at which an article is finished and the date at which it is sold.*

When he reckons on the article he is to produce, he includes in his cost of production, (*a*) the cost of the raw material, (*b*) the waste incident in manufacturing, (*c*) the wear and tear of machinery, (*d*) the time labor will have to expend on the article to finish it, (*e*) the money that its time is worth to labor, (*f*) the interest on that money advanced from free capital for the satisfaction of labor's time for the period between the completion of the article and its sale, and (*g*) finally the interest and taxes, insurance and so forth, on the whole capital invested, except the amount advanced from free capital, interest on which has been looked after.

His *profits* then are the amounts he gets for his perfected article over and above these seven specified elements entering into the *cost of production.*

Third: It will be observed that every function performed by free capital is performed only under the expectation that full satisfaction for this work will be met when the *cost of production is covered.* If satisfaction is not rendered in this way, free capital must disappear. It acts simply as an agent, production being the principal. If production ceases, free capital cannot longer perform its functions. Hence it seems to me that present production is not only the source of present wages, but it is also the source, in the last analysis, of the present free capital associated in production. Under such circumstances it leads only to confusion to multiply terms on this subject.

IT IS AN AFTER-EVENT.

The manufacturer then considers what his building and plant will cost him, what his product will net him, and what funds he would best keep in bank to maintain credit and to meet expenses between manufacture and sale. So far as there being any distinct wages fund, any more than there is any distinct wages fund, or any distinct raw materials fund, or any distinct interest and insurance fund, I cannot concede it. A certain amount of money created by production is expended on each account. It does not originate in capital though advanced by it, but does come from production. The wages of employees are not *predetermined* for a particular time by an absolute law, inevitable, irrevocable, which takes no account of circumstances.

If production is profitable, and suitable labor is scarce, wages will be high. If production is profitable and suitable labor is abundant, wages will be lower, but in that case the wages is determined for that time, not by the amount of circulating capital but by the goods labor can best produce under the existing demand. Wages in all respects depends upon production for what it is.

A manufacturer cannot, outside the law of supply and demand, "set apart" any definite portion of his circulating capital to the payment of wages. He cannot know what he will have to pay for wages until he either actually attempts to employ labor, or until he has made inquiry as to what he can get the required labor for. Therefore, it seems to me that if there is any "wages fund," it is the total amount of money that is paid, not what MUST be paid for labor; that this fund is an *effect* not a *cause;* that it is dependent on the supply and demand of labor; that it is large or small according to the condition of the market and of the labor,—that in short it is the *cart after, but not before the horse.* As such it is not to be considered as an economic "law," for it is not a law of force, it is at most only an event.

CHAPTER X.

WHAT IS MEANT BY DIMINISHING RETURNS.

A Demonstration by Tables of the Absurdity of the so-called Wages Fund Theory — The Foolishness of Applying Foreign Theories to American Conditions of Life — Man's Productiveness Determines his Wages.

———

Our circulating capital in this country does not begin to increase proportionately with our population, and yet wages is not reduced per man, either nominally or in purchasing power, in proportion to this relative increase of population over capital, and will not, before we reach the period of "diminishing returns."

In order to understand this matter thoroughly as respects a new country, I must explain to you what is called the theory of "diminishing returns."

THE THEORY OF "DIMINISHING RETURNS.

In such a country five men settle with their families upon fifty acres of land, clear it, plant it and live out of it. From time to time other men join them until ten men are operating these acres. These ten men will produce, if they are equally industrious and capable, and the land will as readily

respond to labor, twice as much as the five men
did, but by and by the limit of possible proportionate increase of production has been reached on
this fifty acres. Then, owing to more or less
exhaustion of the soil, if another man comes into
the community he cannot add one-tenth to the production from this land, but he produces *something*,
it may be one-fortieth or one-twentieth as much as
one man equally industrious and capable could produce in the earlier years of the farm's history; and
in this case whatever he produces goes to the credit
of the production of the farm.   Let me illustrate
by a table, one hundred being the maximum that
can be produced on this land:

5 men	50 acres	production 40
10 men	50 acres	production 80
12½ men	50 acres	production 100

Now we have reached the maximum of the possible proportionate production of these fifty acres
by 12½ men.   Henceforward we meet with what
we call "diminishing returns."

20 men	50 acres	production 95
30 men	50 acres	production 90
40 men	50 acres	production 80
50 men	50 acres	production 50

The point were the returns are said to diminish,
—that is where one man can no longer produce
one-fifth as much as five or one-tenth as much as
ten,—is reached when the fifty acres of ground are

cultivated by 12½ men. Now then we can add more men to the community but we do not *proportionately* increase the production; yet the production is increased to a certain amount, as will be seen by the table above, though it takes as the land grows older fifty men to produce about what originally five men produced.

This is in brief the history of land cultivation in all countries. There is an increase in the labor force and decrease in the relative productiveness of the land, and of course an accumulating of capital to a certain point. If the population increases much faster than capital and productive opportunities do, there will come a time when the land will not sustain the people on it.

In a new country where we find limited capital and abundant opportunities for labor, immigrants are invited; if they have capital, so much the better. If they have none they are still welcome because the country is so fertile that in a short time they can become productive factors in the community, and after a time accumulate and add to the fixed and circulating capital of the land. If the wages fund theory is correct, every new immigrant would be looked upon with suspicion by the inhabitants unless he brought a large amount of capital with him. For he would increase the divisor, the dividend remaining the same, and consequently the average wages of every man in the community

would be cut down by his coming.   If this rule is
correct, this country has been developed directly in
opposition to it.

As I have stated a number of times in this conversation, the circumstances controlling economic
questions in this new country are entirely different
from what they are in the old countries.   *This
wages fund theory was spun under circumstances
which prevail in the old world under circumstances
of "diminishing returns."*

Labor is in the market like any other exchangeable thing, and it fluctuates according to the same
laws as the price of wheat does, and not according
to its ratio with the circulating capital in the land.

PAUL: What are the "supply" and "demand"
of which you speak with reference to labor?

FATHER: Demand is desire for production,
present or contemplated, inviting an exchange of
labor and wages.   Supply is labor inviting an
exchange of wages for services in production.

You do not fully understand how wages, according to the wages fund theory, is affected when the
period of diminishing returns is reached?   Well,
listen.

*Bear this in mind: The wages fund theorists hold
that all the circulating capital not devoted to raw
material, divided by all the wages workers, gives us
for the time being the fixed, average wages.   Now,
then, for an examination of this theory:*

I. Let me present a table in which *each man
brings an* EQUAL AMOUNT *of Ability and Capital:*

        5   men, 50 acres, production 40, capital $100.00
       10   men, 50 acres, production 80, capital 200.00
      12½   men, 50 acres, production 100, capital 250.00

We have reached the fullest possible production,
with 12½ men on 50 acres of land, and the capital
each man has put in is $20, or $250. Supposing
$100 of the $250 is fixed—in implements, horses,
bonds, etc., we have $150 to divide as wages.
Dividing $150 by 12½ we have $12 as the wages
each averages. Clear, so far, is it not?

II. Well, let me present a table in which *part of
the men bring* NO CAPITAL, *though the Skill and
Ability of each are Equal:*

        5   men, 50 acres, production 40, capital $100.00
       10   men, 50 acres, production 80, capital 180.00
      12½   men, 50 acres, production 100, capital 210.00

If the same part of the capital becomes fixed as
before, there is left $110 to divide into wages for
12½ men, giving an average of less than $9 to
each. The man without capital ought surely not
to be welcomed into a community under such circumstances if the wages fund theory is true, ought
he? But, you notice, the 12½ men still get the
full production from the land, although, by the
table, there is $20 less of capital than in the first
case, but the same labor.

Instead of getting less, however, the history of this country will show, I think, that until the point of diminishing returns is reached, labor gets more rather than less when its productive power is increased by added strength.

III. Another table now, *showing Equal Capital to each and* UNEQUAL ABILITY AND SKILL *in labor:*

> 5   men, 50 acres, production 40. capital $100.00
> 10   men, 50 acres, production 75, capital 200.00
> 12½ men, 50 acres, production 92, capital 250.00

Now we have 12½ men with $250 capital, falling short 8 points of the full production of the 50 acres. Five men make a production of 8 each, but 12½ men are averaging only 7-36 or what 11½ men ought to do. Here production is reduced by incompetency distributed among the last 7½ men, and yet, according to the wages fund theory, the same amount of wages is averaged — *i. e.* $12 *per capita,* because the number of wages workers (12½) dividing $150, makes an average of $12 each!

I insist, to the contrary, that each man's productiveness as a worker fixes his wages, not the amount of capital he does or does not contribute to the community.

IV. Again:

> 5   men, 50 acres, production 40, capital $100.00
> 10   men, 50 acres, production 75, capital 210.00
> 12½ men, 50 acres, production 92, capital 275.00

Here we have *less Industry and more Capital.*
According to the wages fund theory, we shall have
$175 instead of $150 to divide, giving 12½ men —
the last 7½ of whom are inefficient compared with
the first 5,—$14 each! Is not this a reduction of
the theory to an absurdity? Less Industry (not less
labor) more Capital and greater average of wages!

Permit me to renew my somewhat iterated
remark: I dissent from this dismal theory, insisting
that wages arises from production and not from
any part of capital.

V. Let the table be continued from 12½ on to
show the effect in the period of " diminishing returns,"
in which, notwithstanding the decreased proportionate returns there is an increase of capital, both
because it is necessary in order to do the best
farming, and because, by long practice of economy
there is a greater saving every year.

    20 men, 50 acres, production 95, capital $ 400.00
    40 men, 50 acres, production 80, capital   1,000.00
    50 men, 50 acres, production 50, capital   2,000.00
    60 men, 50 acres, production 40, capital   5,000.00

Now among 60 men having a capital of $5,000,
of which $3,000 is devoted to wages, we have an
average of $50 *per capita* in wages, and yet these
sixty men do not get out of the land any more in
the aggregate than the five men got from it. Their
wages, however, is over four times as much as was
averaged by the first five settlers. I hold that

each man working the 50 acres would be robbing capital if he took more as wages from the land than he produces on it.   In this condition each man adds *something* to the production of the sixty, and his coming does not of necessity cut down *by one-sixtieth* the wages of all the rest,

VI. If we have 50,000,000 people, 500,000,000 acres, each producing to full capacity, and a circulating capital of $20,000,000,000, of which $12,-000,000,000 constitutes this so-called wages fund, then the average wages will be $1,400.

VII. If the population and capital are the same, and production has diminished one-half, the average wages is still $1,400, according to the fixed fund theory.

VIII. If population doubles and capital remains the same, whether production increases or decreases, according to this theory the average is but $700!

The wages fund theorists as stated above hold that the population (wages workers) is the divisor, that the part of circulating capital left after the raw material is purchased is the dividend, and by dividing the latter by the former the average of wages for the time being is found.   They do not give production any representation in this example in common division.   The thing seems absurd to me, very!   I believe the sound theory is the one that I have stated, that wages begins in, rises, falls and ceases with production.

IX. The rule in a progressive country is, increase of population and capital, decrease of wages and interest, and decrease in the *proportionate* (but not in the *aggregate*) productiveness of land. What a man can earn by labor on land, in the last analysis, is the base line of the current rate of wages, for, if free to act, he will not accept as wages less from any industry than he can wrest from nature by tillage of the soil. Hence, we find in old countries, wages, having a lower base line to start from, average lower, other things being equal, than in a new country, where nature is very generous to requite even easy toil, and where, consequently, the standard of wages is high. Here again, you see, it is what a man can produce in this, that or the other industry that determines his wages, and not any so-called wages fund.

CHAPTER XI.

THE TWO THEORIES DEMONSTRATED.

THE FALLACY OF THE WAGES FUND THEORY SET FORTH IN A TABLE—HOW WAGES, DEPENDENT ON PRODUCTION, VARY WITH IT.

FATHER: I have put what I think is a demonstration of the fallacy of the wages fund theory into tabular form. In looking over this table please remember that whenever I have doubled the labor on the 50 acres, I have had to add something to the fixed capital, as more implements, etc., are required for say ten men than five, presumably twice as many provided they are all used at the same time; but by doubling the labor we are able the better to subdivide the work so that all shall not be doing the same kind of work at the same time, and hence will not want double the implements. For this reason, where labor is doubled I add only 50 per cent. (see VI. table I.) to the amount of capital fixed in farm implements. When five men, however, double production, I increase by 50 per cent. the capital fixed in implements (see II. in table I.), for it is evident that five men cannot double production without increasing facilities somewhat.

I include, in fixed capital on the farm, the implements, tools, teams, wagons, etc., and then as
only seed is raw material, it is so small an item that
I do not separate it. Furthermore, for the sake of
simplifying the discussion, I assume that title to
the 50 acres has been secured by conquest, pre-
emption or squatter sovereignty. Therefore all
capital is used for implements, etc., and for advancing wages.

In the first exhibit wages is a *sort of dog under
the master's table* which takes what is left after
every other demand is satisfied. In the exhibit I
propose, wages eats at the table with the master and
shares the best of every course!

Now study these two exhibits. They will bear
a good bit of comparison and investigation in con-
nection with our previous discussions of this matter:

I.

WAGES, ACCORDING TO THE WAGES FUND THEORY, INDEPENDENT OF PRODUCTION.

	Labor.	Acres.	Production.	Per Man.	Capital.	Fixed.	Wages Fund.	Average Wages.	Per cent. of Cap.	Per cent. of Wages Fund.	
I	5 Men	50	40	8	100	40	60	12	12	20	⎫
II	5 "	50	**80**	16	100	*60*	40	**8**	8	20	⎪
III	5 "	50	40	8	200	40	160	**32**	16	20	⎪ Production Progressive.
IV	5 "	50	**80**	16	200	80	120	**24**	12	20	⎪
V	10 "	50	40	4	100	*60*	40	**4**	4	10	⎪
VI	10 "	50	**80**	8	100	*60*	40	**4**	4	10	⎬
VII	10 "	50	40	4	200	*60*	140	**14**	7	10	⎪
VIII	10 "	50	**80**	8	200	*60*	140	**14**	7	10	⎪
IX	10 "	50	40	4	*150*	*60*	90	**9**	9	10	⎪
X	10 "	50	40	4	*90*	*a50*	40	**4**	4	10	⎪
XI	12½	50	**100**	8	**250**	100	150	**12**	5	8	⎭
XII	50 "	50	50	1	1000	400	600	**12**	..		⎫ Production Diminishes.
XIII	50 "	50	50	1	1000	600	*b*400	**8**	..		⎬
XIV	.....							..	..		⎭

a. With deficiency of capital I assume they could put less into implements, etc.

b. The further one gets from the period of maximum production, the more of capital must go into machines, implements, etc., to secure even the production that is obtained.

II.

Now for a demonstration, by table, of the counter theory:

WAGES AS DEPENDENT ON PRODUCTION.

	Labor.	Acres.	Production.	Per Man.	Capital.	Per cent. of Wages to Prod.	Wages.	Average to Each.	
1	5 Men	50	40	8	100	75	30	$6.	
2	5 "	50	80	16	100	65	52	10.40	Progressive
3	5 "	50	100	20	100	60	60	12.	Production.
4	10 "	50	80	8	200	60	48	4.80	
5	10 "	50	100	10	200	60	60	6.	
6	12½	50	100	8	250	50	50	4.	Max. Prod'tion
7	20 "	50	95	4.75	400	45	43	2.15	Dim. Returns.
8	40 "	50	80	2	1000	40	32	.80	
9	50 "	50	50	1	1000	30	15	.30	

This exhibit is true, relatively, whatever the conditions of supply and demand for goods or grain may be. I have graduated the per cent. of wages to production from 75 per cent. to 30. I fancy that I have put it too high—but this is immaterial —the table illustrates relations.

In this table you can very readily see how productive power, *regardless of capital at command*, plays hide and seek with wages. For instance (No. 4), labor ·is abundant, and so is capital, but it is not the most productive kind of labor, hence wages

is low, $4.80. Again (No. 3), labor is scarce, but
it is of the highest grade, producing the maximum,
and we have, as might be expected, the highest
wages. In No. 9, labor is abundant, very abundant,
capital is very plentiful, production is at the lowest
ebb, and, as seems proper, wages is on the *rock*.

My son, I leave these tables with you for your
consideration. I have spent more time on this
subject than I intended, but the wages fund theory
makes such a dismal science of political economy
that I feel as if I ought to expose its fallacies to you.

CHAPTER XII.

THE TARIFF, SUBSIDIES AND BOUNTIES.

TARIFF DUTIES PAID BY THE WELL-TO-DO — INTERNAL REV-
ENUE PAID BY THE WAGES EARNERS — POWER TO TAX
UNLIMITED — TARIFF MORE DIRECT AND PREFERABLE TO
SUBSIDIES AND BOUNTIES — GROWTH OF "FAIR TRADE"
SENTIMENT IN GREAT BRITAIN — RUINOUS BELGIAN COM-
PETITION — COMPARATIVE ENGLISH AND MASSACHUSETTS
WAGES.

PAUL: The protective tariff is a tax, plus interest thereon, which is eventually paid by the consumer. This you admit?

FATHER: Yes, and our internal revenue taxes are *paid by the consumer*, though many of them are *so disguised that the consumer is not conscious that he is contributing unto Cæsar*.

PAUL: Has the government the right to levy taxes except for revenue?

FATHER: That right has been exercised since 1789 in this country as a function of the general government.

PAUL: Can government tax a thing out of existence?

FATHER: The theory is that the power to tax, if it exist at all, is unlimited. I do not like this view of it. It is a dangerous prerogative, this

power to tax unto death, but it must be admitted
that when you concede that the government has a
right to tax for other purposes than for revenue,
you place no limitation to that power—the only
limitation, if it may be so called, residing in
the discretion of the law-making and law-confirm-
ing powers.

WHY A TARIFF IS PREFERABLE TO SUBSIDIES AND BOUNTIES.

Our government from the first was committed to
protection and it adopted a tariff therefor instead
of subsidies and bounties, and I am inclined to
think that *a judicious tariff distributes advantages
better than would bounties and subsidies* such as
Great Britain extends to many of her favorite
industries. These too are taxes paid by the consumer and theoretically are open to quite as many
objections from a free trade standpoint as are
protective duties. The more direct taxation is,
the less inequalities prevail. *A protective tariff is
paid by the well-to-do classes* who will import what
they want at whatever cost; whereas internal revenue is an indirect tax which is *paid by the wages
earners* as a matter of necessity. In this country
we get the bulk of our revenue from the tariff; * in
Great Britain there is no tariff except on spirits,

* For year ending July 1, 1887, the customs duties receipts were
$217,286,893 and the internal revenue receipts $118,823,391.

tobacco, tea, coffee, and a few such articles, the bulk of the expenses of government being raised by the indirect inland revenue tax which almost nothing escapes. As the tariff therefore comes out of the pockets of the rich and extravagant and is more direct than would be subsidies and bounties, to which all the people would, by the indirect taxation of internal revenue, contribute, and which would be much higher were this form of governmental assistance the rule, I think *the true protective tariff works less injustice and is easier borne than any other accepted form of assistance.*

FAIR TRADE SENTIMENT.

Great Britain, you see, is not an absolutely free trade country because she levies duties on certain articles and *always puts a higher duty on the manufactured article than on the raw material*, thus practicing the very essence of protection; and there is a strong sentiment developing among her manufacturers in favor of what they call "fair trade," that is, trade protected by duties when necessary, for the English manufacturer is often underbid in his own territory on work in which he has been reputed to excel, by Belgian manufacturers, who can compete with him successfully because *wages are lower in Belgium than they are in England.* Sir George Elliot, M. P., one of the largest coal miners and iron manufacturers of Great Britain, told me that his own class of manufacturers was underbid by Belgian iron men on the contract for one of the largest railway stations in England, and secured the job, and such instances are multiplying every day. They emphasize the lesson that there is reason and common sense in a fair trade or protective policy when in an unqualified free trade policy there may be ruinous competition from abroad. I did not intend to quote any statistics, but to show you how much lower relative wages are in England and Massachusetts let me read you the following: "In the fall of 1883," says Carroll D. Wright, Commissioner of Massachusetts, "we started upon an original investigation through personal agents of the bureau, in Massachusetts and Great Britain, and through these agents we have gathered from original sources (meaning by original sources the pay-rolls of great manufacturing establishments, the official wages lists agreed upon in England, so far as England is concerned, between trade societies and employers, and from other reliable sources) the rate of wages paid in the following twenty-four industries which are common to Massachusetts and Great Britain:

RATE OF WAGES PAID IN INDUSTRIES COMMON

TO MASSACHUSETTS AND GREAT BRITAIN.

INDUSTRIES, 1884.	General Average Weekly Wages Paid to all Employees.	
	Massachusetts.	Great Britain.
Agricultural implements...............	$10.25	$8.85
Artisans' tools......................	11.80	4.89
Boots and shoes.....................	11.63	4.37
Bricks	8.63	4.16
Building trades.....................	14.99	7.21
Carpetings	6.08	4.11
Carriages and wagons................	13.80	4.89
Clothing............................	10.01	6.71
Cotton goods........................	6.45	4.66
Flax and jute goods.................	6.46	2.84
Food preparations...................	9.81	2.72
Furniture...........................	11.04	7.96
Glass...............................	12.28	6.94
Hats — fur, wool and silk............	11.01	5.51
Hosiery.............................	6.49	4.67
Liquors, malt and distilled.........	12.87	12.66
Machines and machinery..............	11.75	6.93
Metals and metallic goods...........	11.25	7.40
Printing and publishing.............	11.37	5.52
Printing, dyeing, bleaching, and finishing cotton textiles.........................	8.67	4.94
Stone...............................	14.39	8.58
Wooden goods........................	12.19	5.67
Woolen goods........................	6.90	4.86
Worsted goods.......................	7.32	3.60
All industries average	$10.31	$5.86

By this comparison you will observe that were
free trade established between Great Britain and

Massachusetts, the former, in the matter of the wages alone of the industries named, would have a tremendous competing advantage over the old Bay State, *notwithstanding the fact that American labor is from* 25 *to* 33⅓ *per cent. more productive than any foreign labor.* As wages are somewhat lower in Massachusetts than they are in the entire United States, the result would be more disastrous to the entire country than with Massachusetts.

PART III.

Capital, Labor, Strikes, Arbitration, Profit Sharing, etc., etc.

.

___

CHAPTER XIII.

RELATIONS BETWEEN CAPITAL AND LABOR.

DEFINITIONS — TRADE ORGANIZATIONS JUSTIFIABLE —"TAKES TWO TO MAKE A BARGAIN"— ALIENATIONS THAT ARE FOOLISH — A DUEL.— MATERIAL INTERESTS ARE SAFE IN THE HANDS OF HONEST WORKINGMEN.

___

PAUL: If you are so disposed, father, I would like to discuss the question of the relations of capital and labor. We hear a good deal about antagonism existing between them — a sort of "irrepressible conflict," and many people look forward, I am told, to the future of these relations with no small apprehension.

FATHER: What is capital? What is labor? These questions first require an answer. Financial capital is profit of production reserved for future production. Labor is the service which capital must have in order to secure further production.

EXPERIENCE, ETC., NOT CAPITAL.

Some writers and thinkers use the term capital somewhat loosely, I think, when they speak of a literary man's intellectual ability and the expert's acumen as capital. I do not so regard them. They probably belong to the department of skilled labor — their possession enhances the value of the literary man's work and the expert's services, but they can scarcely be called capital because they are not tangible; they cannot be taxed; they cannot be loaned to another for monetary consideration; they are not impaired or enhanced by changes in commercial conditions. They are of no value without the stimulus of financial capital. Like labor, unless demanded by capital, they do not yield any return to the possessor.

In all economic discussion, we greatly simplify matters by simply defining our terms, and therefore I exclude intelligence, skill, experience, etc., from the domain of capital and place them in the category of labor.

CAPITAL THE CHILD OF LABOR AND INTELLIGENCE.

Capital is an accumulation of property or funds resulting from past labor and intelligence — literally a son of sorrow and toil. It is the organization of commercial force. The purpose of its organization is to increase itself. As it is born of intelligent labor, it cannot grow without the assistance of labor. Capital that is unproductive soon disappears—it feeds on its own vitals. Furthermore we must not forget that capital is organized on the purely selfish basis like every other human commercial force. It is always looking out for "Number One," and must necessarily do so else it would soon disappear from the earth.

PAUL: Would this be a calamity? Is not the organization of capital a menace?

FATHER: It would indeed be a calamity if capital were swept from the earth because then labor would be reduced to beggary—and beggary which would cry aloud in vain, for there would be no hand to help, no arm to save. Better the deluge, wherein all might perish at once, than such a catastrophe!

Yes, the tendency of capital, just as the tendency of democracy, is towards centralization of power, and irresponsibility, but it is amenable to public opinion and can be held in check.

ORGANIZATIONS OF CAPITAL AND LABOR.

Now then, for illustrations: In our primitive community, a capital of $100,000 was collected for the plow works and negotiations were opened for services of needed labor. It is plain that capital must pay labor fully as much as labor could obtain from any other employment it could find. If the only other occupation of the people was agriculture, capital must reward the services of labor to the same extent,—either by money or its equivalent in more agreeable kinds of work —that the same amount of intelligence and skill devoted to agriculture would produce. If the demand for the labor it wanted exceeded the supply of such labor, capital would have to pay a larger amount in order to induce labor to offer desired service. If such service was very scarce, of course the extra wages inducement would increase the cost of production, which must be met either by charging, if possible, a higher price for the plows, or capital must be content with a smaller per centum of profit.

In the earlier history of capital associated for manufacture, labor is scarce and is able to drive a better bargain for its services, and unless later on labor organizes itself as capital has done, the tendency of time is to make labor more dependent and capital more dictatorial.

Mark me, my son, neither labor nor capital can, by organization alone, increase its relative value. Organization can simply render them more certain against imposition for one reason: *"It takes two to make a bargain"; and I insist upon it that the capitalist alone is not to be trusted always to do exact justice by labor.* Furthermore, labor is not qualified to estimate exactly its value to capital. *We cannot take it for granted that without some sort of compulsion men will be just and square with their fellows,* whether they are capitalists or laborers.

PAUL: Then I suppose you believe in the thousand and one organizations of workingmen?

TRADE ORGANIZATIONS LEGITIMATE.

FATHER: Certainly I do so far as these organizations are formed for the purpose of resisting the tendency of capital to become unjustifiably dictatorial and irresponsible. *They have a good reason for existence but it requires a very great degree of wisdom in their management to restrain them from extreme and unjustifiable proceedings* — a tendency which is very great because there are many times when labor in adversity gets desperate, when it hears the howl of the wolf of hunger not afar off. *Labor has rights which capital is bound to respect,* and it is because capital has not respected these rights as tenderly as it ought to have done, it is because capital has organized sometimes for protection and sometimes for aggression that organizations of labor have sprung into being. *Capital, too, has rights which labor is bound to respect.* They have mutual interests inside and outside the boundaries of their "inalienable rights," and when they both recognize and respect these rights, *the apparent conflict between them becomes a sort of individual affair — not a positive hostility between the two great commercial divisions of mankind.*

The self-seeking meddlers on both sides are responsible, chiefly, for the wrangles that do occur. But to illustrate by a little —

FANCY SKETCH OF A DUEL.

John Honest and Henry Caput had grown up together as boys. Both had sprung from obscure parentage, and neither was able to tell the fate of the father or mother. Occasional stories had come to their ears that they were related to each other, but the evidence was so cloudy that they paid no attention to it. As children they were devoted to each other, but as they grew up they showed a disposition towards what was at first friendly rivalry in sports and employments. They were of equal height and people often remarked that "they look near enough alike to be brothers." John became a shoemaker in his native place and was as honest as the day. While his education was limited his common sense was strong and he was looked upon as a leader among his fellows and was at the head of the labor society of the town.

Henry, when he became of age, sought his fortune in California gold mines, and after years of hardships and suffering returned to his native town a rich man. He soon acquired elegant tastes, drove nice horses, was fond of the good things of life, and yet withal was a generous friend of the charities and benevolences of his native town and gave large amounts of money to beautify and adorn it.

He had many fawning courtiers about him, unthinking, unreasonable men, one of whom sought to poison his mind against his old friend John Honest, who he said was circulating evil reports about him and organizing his friends to prevent him from gaining any success in his future financial efforts. Busybodies on the other side poisoned John's mind against Henry, and these old friends became sworn enemies.

One day they met on the public street, hot words were exchanged — John calling Henry a thief and a robber and Henry intimating that John was a coward and a sneak.

A challenge followed.

To nerve each man for the contest, the seconds shaved off their beards, and daubed their faces with lampblack, fearing that the old associations of friendship would unman them unless they were disguised, and prevent the "satisfaction" each sought in gore.

The fatal day came. The men stood before each other for the word, great beads of sweat pouring down their faces obscuring their sight. Each simultaneously wiped with his arm his sweaty face,— the daubs went with the sweat!

The beardless faces thus uncovered were the faces of the boys of twenty years ago — boys who had loved each other.

The duel incontinently ended.

D

The next week an old and toil-worn man came
to the town and through him it was learned beyond a doubt that John and Henry were brothers!

And so it is the busybodies, the lazy good-for-
nothings, the scandal-mongers, the incendiaries,
who are seeking to involve John Labor and Henry
Capital in conflict — they who are sons of the same
parents, who spent their youth together, and whose
manhood, whatever their circumstances, should be
one of amity and mutual respect.

Evils move along the line of least resistance,
and because capital has so long been organized
and labor has so long scattered its forces, capital
has gradually begun to think itself greater than
everything else in society and irresponsible — an
error which the organization of labor will undoubtedly correct by a counter influence on public opinion.   To get this influence, labor must be wise,
conservative and just in all its doings and demands.

PAUL: Are the relations between organized
capital and organized labor amicable ?

FATHER: I think each is suspicious of the
other. For years labor was in abject subjection
unto capital, and is so in some of the older countries to-day. In England when labor began to
combine into trades unions against the influence
of dictatorial capital, the organizations were out-
lawed. This was a false step — it was overreach-
ing and of course it drove the members of the

unions to excesses which probably would never
otherwise have been committed. The very fact of
the organization of these unions would be proof to
the social economist that there was a good reason
for their evolution, but like all checks to tyranny,
they met with a baptism of fire and persecution.
Their function was desired, and their excesses
would not have been committed had they not been
confronted with a hostile public opinion created in
a large measure by organized capital.

A HEALTHFUL EVOLUTION.

Since 1870 trades unionism has flourished in the
United States. In 1877, some fiery spirits brought
some discredit on the organizations, but I believe
when they cling simply to their "inalienable rights"
of self-defense against oppression; when they overcome any tendency to interfere with those who
do not act in unison with them; when they rely
entirely upon the justness of their cause rather than
upon the un-American "boycott," they are in harmony with the spirit of American institutions; that,
conducted with prudence, they have and deserve
public countenance, and that they can be of very
material benefit to the trades whose interests they
seek to serve.

SAFEGUARDS AGAINST ANARCHISTS.

In my opinion they are the very best safeguards
we have against anarchists who threaten such dire-

ful things. Our interests can be in no safer hands than in the hands of the honest, intelligent, liberty-loving American workingmen. I do not believe that they can be used by plotters against the public peace. Their membership is made up of the bone and sinew of the country, of the strong, common-sensible people, who have the wisdom to resist as well the attempt of terrorists to use them, as of the other extreme to abuse them and traduce their motives and acts. I have no fear of them — I have infinitely more fear of the out-of-sight organizations of men who despise public opinion and who by bribery and corruption seek to ride roughshod over the rights of the people.

The process of evolution has not yet given us, perhaps, an ideal trades unionism, but the future will disclose it, and when all present crudities and malformed features are removed, we shall find in these organizations an element of very desirable politico-social strength. Confidence and mutual respect will succeed suspicion, and organized capital and organized labor will be rivals but not of necessity enemies. Each will get all it can out of the bargain which it negotiates.

ULTIMATE GOOD FROM STRIKES.

PAUL: Then I suppose you approve of strikes?

FATHER: Not necessarily. The spirit which has caused strikes has its root in a defense of rights, but unless one knows all the circumstances of the case, one can pronounce no definite opinion on the merit of individual proceedings.

It cannot be denied that fear of a strike against injustice has a salutary influence against undue greed on the part of capital, and though the present effect of a "strike" may be disastrous, I do not doubt that needed material good is evolved from it.

ARBITRATION COMMENDED.

Yes, my son, I would strongly recommend arbitration. The same or a better result is reached by it and both labor and capital suffer less loss.

CHAPTER XIV.

LABOR AND CAPITAL SHARING PROFITS.

SALUTARY RESULTS OF THIS FORM OF CO-OPERATION — STIMULATING MANFUL SELF-INTEREST ON BEHALF OF CAPITAL.

PAUL: What further can you suggest in the way of bringing capital and labor into more intimate relations? I have no doubt, as you say, that their interests are mutual, but they do not seem to be at all tender of each other. I may be young and shortsighted, but I rather like the manufacturer so closely described in "John Halifax, Gentleman." It seems to me that more such characters ought to be met with in daily life. Do you not think well of co-operation?

FATHER: Co-operation in the purchase of the necessities of life seems to be satisfactory when fully tried. Individuals are thus given the benefit of wholesale rates plus the expenses of management, and I approve it. Co-operation in manufacturing is not so simple, nor is it I fancy so satisfactory. If fifty men put together all the capital they can raise and go into the manufacture of plows I doubt very much if they will succeed as well as would a single firm of one or two persons in the conduct of the business.

Business like an army must have a head and competent subordinates to take advantage of all the points which an ever-changing market presents. Of course a co-operative concern can put its affairs into the hands of one or two or three executives but even then I doubt if there is the element of stability and continuity of a prudent policy in them that we expect to find in private centralized firms and companies.

PROFIT SHARING AMONG WAGES EARNERS.

Personally I think very highly of the plan of capital giving labor a per centum of its profits over and above a certain stipulated figure. This plan enlists one's self-interest as no other known plan does, and you will find, my son, that there is nothing which so interests a workingman in his employment as the idea or hope of a proprietary share in the success of his employers. Under such a plan the men are more hopeful; they look forward to a future of some promise; they feel—they know— their employer's interests are also their own. I wonder why this plan is not more generally adopted.

PAUL: Is this plan successful when tried?

FATHER: I am told that it is. Many large jobbing houses in the country have adopted it, and even when they have put their desired profit at a high figure, it is said that the zeal inspired in the beneficiaries of the plan has been so great that this profit has been realized and a large amount in addition secured for division among the percentum employees. Under this plan the employees share in the profits above a certain figure—say 15 per cent.—but they do not bear their share of the losses which are sometimes heavy and inevitable spite of the wisest management. But I dare say that the firm practicing this sort of business will seldom —it ought never to—meet with any opposition if a reduction of wages or a cessation of production is found necessary.

PAUL: Do you think that all the labor employed should be a beneficiary under this plan?

FATHER: I think an interest in profits should surely be given to those whose fidelity and worth have been shown in extended service. I am satisfied, however, that if the plan were extended even to all the labor employed, it would yield the most satisfactory returns, and establish relations between capital and labor that would be in the highest degree beneficial.

PAUL: But would not this plan necessarily presuppose a lower rate of wages in an establishment conducted on the division of profits?

FATHER: Not necessarily.

PAUL: Would not the part divided with labor necessarily come out of the pockets of capital?

FATHER: No, not unless you can show beyond a doubt that without such a division or distribution capital would gain as much as or more than it does under it. I think this could not be proved, for the reason stated above. Better and more faithful service is stimulated by the limited partnership plan; capital gets the degree of profit it desires and the employees secure all the surplus their energy can gain for the concern. Wages, moreover, being paid for from the products of present industry, if this plan promotes productiveness of labor, and the market for the wares made remains good, wages ought to be higher and better assured under what I may call this limited partnership plan.

CHAPTER XV.

COMPARATIVE STATISTICS.

The United States Leads all Competitors in Manufactures, Wealth, etc.—Sixty-six Per Cent. of Population Diverted into Productive Industries—Under a Free Trade Policy England would use us as a Surplus Market—Tariff Matters Must be Regulated by Good Business Sagacity and Common Sense.

FATHER: Figures sometimes are more eloquent than all theories. It may be well, therefore, to show some of the results of economic policies practiced by different nations. I give first the total manufactures of the leading nations, in 1880:

United States.............................$4,440,000,000
Great Britain........ 3,790,000,000
France................................... 2,425,000,000
Germany 2,135,000,000
Russia................................... 1,145,000,000
Austria....... 1,030,000,000
Italy 575,000,000

The United States leads the world in manufactures, with free trade (free trade since 1846) England her next competitor, the other nations practicing a protective policy. The value of the total industrial or manufactured products is:

United States........ ....$10,395,000,000
Great Britain 10,120,000,000
France. 6,625,000,000

Germany......................   6,345,000,000
Russia.   4,300,000,900
Austria.   3,285,000,000
Italy.   1,895,000,000

Here, too, the United States leads all the rest.

The following table shows how splendidly, up to 1880, the United States had forged ahead:

	Wealth.	Income.	Debt.	Net Wealth.
United States.....	$47,475	$7,100	$1,842	$45,633
Great Britain.....	43,600	6.235	3,845	39,755
France..........	40,300	4,852	4,555	35,745
Germany........	31,615	4,250	1,145	30,470
Russia..........	21,715	3,800	2,765	18,940
Austria.........	18,065	3,010	2,095	15,970
Italy...........	11,755	1,450	2,610	9,145

These figures represent billions. Here, too, the United States leads all the rest of the world in wealth and income. The average wealth a head in the United States, in 1880, was about $8.70; in Great Britain it was about $9.70.

To show how our laboring force has been distributed: we had in 1880 a total laboring population of 17,392,099, divided according to vocation as follows:

In agriculture.................7,670,493, or 44 per cent.
In professional and personal....4,074,238, or 23½ "   "
In trades and transportation....1,810,256, or 10½ "   "
In manufacturing, mining and
    mechanics...............3,837,112, or 22   "   "

This shows that under the economic policy—the protective—66 per cent. of our working people have been diverted from the tillage of the soil to other industries.

RESULTS, NOT PROOFS.

None of these tables *prove* that protection is a better policy for the United States than free trade, but they do show that under a protective policy we lead the world in total manufactures, in total wealth, in the value of total manufactured or industrial products, and that wonderful and desirable diversity of employments have attended us in our national development. The free trader may say that it does not follow that even better results would not have followed had the free trade policy been pursued, which I may admit, though I doubt it. England has always been an aggressive commercial power and has always usurped every local market the world over as her own by a sort of divine right unless the local market has resisted her assumptions. So aggressive has been her crowding usurping function in this particular that her own colonies all over the world have been compelled to bar her out of their markets by tariffs that she has not been able to override. She always pursued this policy towards this country when we were in the colonial period, and if she had had her own way in shaping our economic policy after we gained our independence, she would have robbed us of the substantial fruits of self-reliant commercial and industrial independence by insisting that this country was naturally an agricultural and pastoral country, that it should cling to its " heaven-designed mission " and buy its manufactures of her own natural and best equipped artisans and mechanics. In the period from 1784 to 1790, without protection, the balance of trade against us and in favor of England was over $50,000,000. From 1795 to 1801, under a protective policy, the balance of trade in our favor and against Great Britain was about $90,000.000, a reversal of $140,000,000.

PAUL: Yes, but did not this extra taxation of our own people check our own material progress?

FATHER: Not demonstrably. We paid the extra price, and thanks to the stimulus given to the erection of new industries, we were able to do so and have a handsome margin, in the bargain.

PAUL: If free trade were made the American policy to-day and we had for example 1,000 independent industries and 250 dependent industries, all having competitors in England, could England probably undersell us in our own markets after bringing her products 3,000 miles?

FATHER: Yes.

PAUL: As respects our independent industries?

FATHER: Yes, sir, as respects all of them if she was disposed so to do.

PAUL: Then what is the use of protection, if, as you say, she could undersell our manufacturers that we had protected to the point of so-called independence?

A SURPLUS MARKET FOR ENGLAND.

FATHER: That's a close question, and well asked. It brings up just the very point that I want to discuss for a few minutes. It doesn't follow that she could always undersell our manufacturers that had been protected up to the point of independence. But if her home and Indian and other exclusive markets were good, she would use the United States if need be for a dumping ground for her surplus products in this way: She could manufacture $2,000,000 worth of steel rails, say, cheaper than she could $1,000,000 worth. If she could dispose of $1,500,000 worth or more at a good profit, say 10 per cent. in all her other accessible markets, she could afford to sell her surplus in the United States at one per cent. profit, or even at cost, yes and a trifle below cost, for in that event she would make an average profit of 10 per cent. less what she might throw off the surplus in the American market. Of course this would paralyze any American steel rail manufactures. Carry this mere imaginary illustration through the entire line of competition, and you can readily see how the American market would soon be in utter depend-

ence upon the schemes of the British manufacturer.
The result would be an immediate destruction of
production, a vast superabundance of labor, a low-
ering and cutting off of wages and the prostration
of the country.

PAUL: But couldn't our manufacturers play the
same game and carry the war into the English
markets?

FATHER: No, not unless we had the same
capacity for cheap production, the same rate of
wages, were content with the same scale of
profits and had the same means of ready and
cheap transportation. Most of these elements we
would never possess until like her we had passed
the point of diminishing returns, and labor expended on land produced no greater results here
than there, for what labor expended in the cultivation of land can produce is the standard of wages
the world over. It produces most in the newest
and least densely-settled country, and hence wages
must be higher in the United States than in England, the profits of business must therefore be
higher unless we can gain compensating advantages in greater industry and better machinery.
This possibility however would be cut off if Great
Britain were allowed to use us for her surplus
market.

A TARIFF FOREVER?

PAUL: Accordingly, you would always have to

AA 001 120 471 6

maintain a tariff if there were any probability that we would become the surplus market?

FATHER: We must always regulate our economic policy by the rivalries which we have to meet. It would never do to adopt any sort of economic policy that ignored destructive competition. As a nation we must exercise the same sagacity that we do as individuals, shape our policy to the circumstances in which we are placed, and in every emergency see to it that if we cannot gain in other respects compensating or retaliatory advantages, we must not open our ports indiscriminately to foreigners.

PAUL: If the whole world were practicing free trade would we not still be in danger of becoming the surplus market?

FATHER: The field of free operation being so much larger, and the older countries of Europe possessing so many coequal advantages with Great Britain, she would not command undisputed so many markets, and her average profits would be so reduced that she could not afford to sell to us at such low prices.

"Each industry is entitled to protection for what it is worth to the community, for if Louisiana, for instance, cannot produce sugar of sufficient quality and quantity to supply the country, the price of what she can produce would be a check upon the price of the foreign product, which would not sell at a higher figure than what the Louisiana sugar could be produced for."

www.ingramcontent.com/pod-product-compliance
Lightning Source LLC
Chambersburg PA
CBHW030537270326
41927CB00008B/1420

* 9 7 8 3 3 3 7 2 3 7 0 9 7 *